Pregnancy Guide for the Journey Together

Essential Insights and Practical Tips for Supporting Your Partner from Conception to Birth

Alexander Hart

© **Copyright 2024 by Alexander Hart - All rights reserved**.

This document is geared towards providing exact and reliable information in regard to the topic and issue covered.

- From a Declaration of Principles which was accepted and approved equally by a Committee of the American Bar Association and a Committee of Publishers and Associations.

In no way is it legal to reproduce, duplicate, or transmit any part of this document in either electronic means or in printed format. All rights reserved.

The information provided herein is stated to be truthful and consistent, in that any liability, in terms of inattention or otherwise, by any usage or abuse of any policies, processes, or directions contained within is the solitary and utter responsibility of the recipient reader. Under no circumstances will any legal responsibility or blame be held against the publisher for any reparation, damages, or monetary loss due to the information herein, either directly or indirectly.

Respective authors own all copyrights not held by the publisher.

The information herein is offered for informational purposes solely and is universal as so. The presentation of the information is without contract or any type of guarantee assurance.

The trademarks that are used are without any consent, and the publication of the trademark is without permission or backing by the trademark owner. All trademarks and brands within this book are for clarifying purposes only and are owned by the owners themselves, not affiliated with this document.

EXTRA BONUS!!!!

EXERCISE AND HEALTHY LIFESTYLE DURING PREGNANCY

READ TO THE END AND SCAN THE QR CODE

Table of contents

1. Introduction 6
2. Understanding Pregnancy 8
   Overview of Pregnancy: Trimesters and Stages 8
   Physical and Emotional Changes in the Partner 10
   Baby's Development Week by Week 12
   Myths and Realities About Pregnancy 14
3. Preparing for Fatherhood 16
   Common Expectations and Fears 16
   Your Mindset: How to Prepare Psychologically 17
   Communicating with Your Partner: Listening and Support 19
   Couple Exercise #1 : Create a List of Expectations and Fears 20
4. Health and Wellness 23
   Importance of Physical and Mental Health for Both 23
   Healthy Eating During Pregnancy 24
   Physical Activity: What to Do and What to Avoid 26
   How to Reduce Stress for You and Your Partner 29
   Couple Exercise #2: Prepare Healthy Meals Together 30
5. Medical Visits and Tests 33
   Overview of Prenatal Visits 33
   Common Tests and Screenings During Pregnancy 34
   How to Actively Participate in Medical Visits 36
   Useful Questions to Ask the Doctor 37
   Couple Exercise #3: Prepare a List of Questions for the Doctor 39
6. Preparing for the Baby's Arrival 42
   Essential Shopping List for the Newborn 42
   Preparing the Baby's Nursery 44
   Birth Planning and Choosing the Hospital 46
   Discussing Birth Plans and Partner's Preferences 48
   Couple Exercise #4: Create a Shopping List Together 50
7. Labor and Postpartum 53
   Signs of Labor and When to Go to the Hospital 53
   Father's Role During Labor and Delivery 54
   Caring for Your Partner After Birth 57
   Involvement in the First Weeks of the Baby's Life 59
   Couple Exercise #5: Discuss and Plan for the Birth Day 61

8. Parenthood and Relationships 63
Strengthening the Couple's Relationship 63
Effective Communication and Conflict Management 65
Dividing Household Tasks and Baby Care 67
Importance of Quality Family Time 69
Couple Exercise #6: Schedule Quality Time Together 71

9. Practical Aspects of Fatherhood 73
Diaper Changing and Feeding the Newborn 73
Sleep Patterns and Managing Sleepless Nights 74
Newborn Safety at Home and Outside 76
Baby Care and Hygiene 78
Couple Exercise #7: Practice Changing a Diaper Together (with a Doll) 80

10. Resources and Support 83
Professional Counseling and Help 83
Recognizing and Addressing Postpartum Depression (for Both Mother and Father) 85
Building a Family and Social Support Network 87
Couple Exercise #8: Find and Join a Local or Online Support Group 89

FAQ 92

Concluding Thoughts and Acknowledgements 94

1. Introduction

Welcome to Future Dads

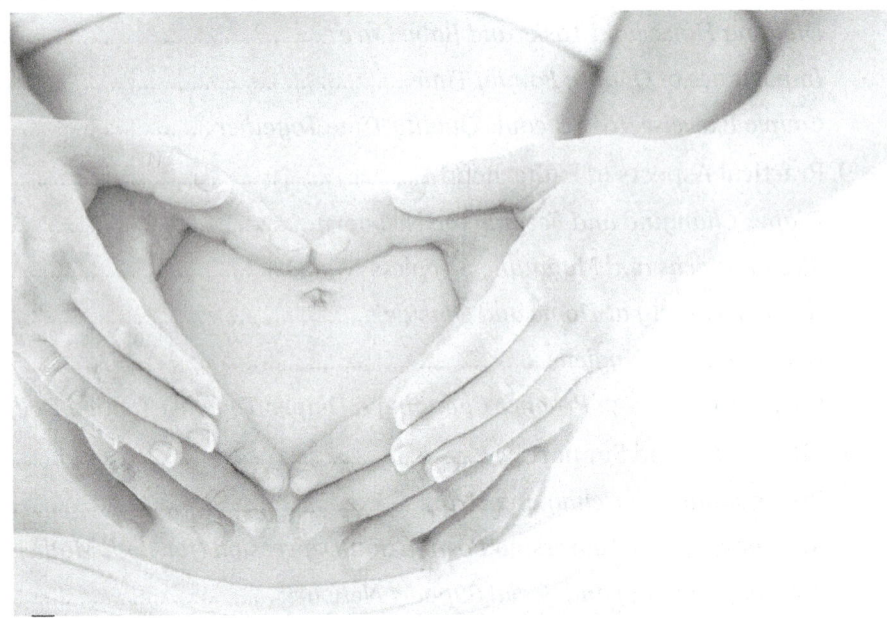

Welcome to this incredible adventure! Whether you are anxiously awaiting the arrival of your first child or are just beginning to consider fatherhood, this guide is here to help you. Becoming a first-time dad is full of emotions, challenges, and unforgettable moments. This book aims to provide practical advice, support and insights to make this transition smoother and more enjoyable.

Objectives of the book

Our goal is to provide you with all the knowledge and tools you need to support your partner during pregnancy and prepare you for the responsibilities and joys of parenthood. We will cover everything from understanding the stages of pregnancy to practical tips for the delivery room to how to be a supportive partner throughout the journey.

How to use this guide

This book is structured to be comprehensive and accessible. You can read it from cover to cover or refer to the sections that interest you most at any time. Each chapter is designed to provide you with practical tips and insights, as well as exercises and suggestions for you and your partner. Keep an eye out for "Frequently Asked Questions" sections, where we address common problems and provide practical solutions.

Brief overview of the book's contents

Here's what you can expect:

- **Understanding Pregnancy**: Learn about the different stages of pregnancy, your partner's physical and emotional changes, and your baby's development week by week.

- **Preparing for parenthood**: Preparing yourself mentally and emotionally, understanding common expectations and fears, and improving communication with your partner.

- **Health and wellness**: Learn the importance of a healthy lifestyle, including diet and exercise, and how to reduce stress for both you and your partner.

- **Medical checkups and examinations**: Learn more about various prenatal visits, exams and screenings during pregnancy and how to actively participate in medical appointments.

- **Preparation for baby's arrival**: get practical advice on preparing the baby's room, creating a birth plan, and discussing preferences with your partner.

- **Labor and postpartum**: understand the signs of labor, your role during birth, and how to care for your partner and baby after birth.

- **Parenting and relationships**: Strengthening the couple relationship, managing household activities and ensuring quality family time.

- **Practical aspects of fatherhood**: Learning how to change diapers, feed the newborn, manage sleep routines, and ensure the baby's safety.

- **Resources and Support**: Finding professional help, recognizing postpartum depression, and building a family and social support network.

Each section is designed to provide not only the necessary information, but also practical exercises to do with your partner. You will thus be able to consolidate the couple and the "Future Parents" team more closely, facing together the joys and concerns of this journey undertaken.

Our tone is encouraging and positive because we believe in the importance of your role as a father. You are about to embark on one of the best journeys of your life, and we are here to help you experience it to the fullest.

With this guide in hand, you will be well prepared to face the challenges and embrace the joys of becoming a father. Let's begin this exciting journey together!

2. Understanding Pregnancy

EMBRYONIC DEVELOPMENT

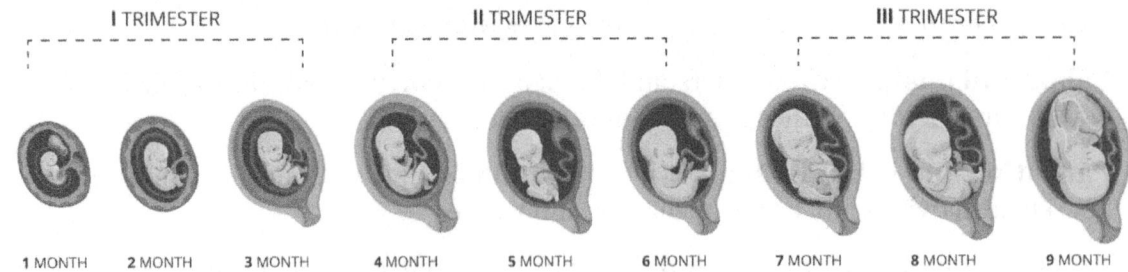

Overview of Pregnancy: Trimesters and Stages

Pregnancy is typically divided into three trimesters, each lasting about three months. Understanding the stages of pregnancy can help you better support your partner and prepare for the changes that come with each phase. Here's an overview of what happens during each trimester:

First Trimester (Weeks 1 to 12)

Development of the Baby:

- **Conception:** Pregnancy begins with the fertilization of an egg by a sperm, forming a zygote.
- **Implantation:** By the end of the first month, the zygote becomes an embryo and implants in the uterine wall.
- **Vital Organs Begin to Form:** The heart, brain, spinal cord, and other organs start to develop.
- **Physical Features:** By the end of the first trimester, the baby's facial features begin to take shape, and tiny limbs start to form.

Changes in the Mother:

- **Hormonal Adjustments:** Significant hormonal changes can affect almost every organ system in the body.
- **Common Symptoms:** Nausea (often called morning sickness), fatigue, frequent urination, and emotional fluctuations are typical.
- **Medical Visits:** Early prenatal visits typically include blood tests, a physical exam, and often the first ultrasound to confirm the pregnancy and check the embryo's health.

How To Support your partner:

- Offer emotional support and understanding as your partner adjusts to the hormonal changes.
- Help manage morning sickness by preparing small, frequent meals.

Second Trimester (Weeks 13 to 26)

Development of the Baby:

- **Growth Spurt:** The fetus undergoes significant growth during this trimester, increasing in size and weight.
- **Sensory Development:** The fetus begins to hear and swallow, and hair begins to grow.
- **Movement:** Movements and kicks become noticeable as muscles and bones strengthen.

Changes in the Mother:

- **Physical Appearance:** The belly becomes more pronounced as the baby grows and the uterus expands.
- **Decrease in Early Symptoms:** Symptoms like nausea tend to decrease, but new ones such as heartburn and abdominal pain may appear.
- **Ultrasound Scans:** Detailed ultrasound scans can check fetal anatomy and development.

How To Support your partner:

- Encourage and participate in physical activities, as it's usually the most comfortable trimester for most women.
- Start planning the nursery and shopping for baby essentials together.

Third Trimester (Weeks 27 to Birth)

Development of the Baby:

- **Preparation for Birth:** The fetus gains more weight, stores fat, and continues to mature its lungs and brain.
- **Positioning:** The fetus moves into a head-down position in preparation for birth.
- **Final Development:** Reflexes are honed, and the fetus can now blink, turn the head, and react to sounds, light, and touch.

Changes in the Mother:

- **Braxton Hicks Contractions:** Occasional contractions may start, which are not real labor but a preparation for it.

- **More Frequent Medical Checks:** Visits to the doctor become more frequent to monitor the health of both mother and fetus.
- **Preparing for Delivery:** Discussions about birth plans and signs of labor become key components of prenatal visits.

How To Support your partner:

- Assist in final preparations, such as packing the hospital bag and installing the baby's car seat.
- Offer physical support, like massages to relieve back pain, and help with mobility.

Understanding these stages will help you empathize with the physical and emotional changes your partner is experiencing and enable you to provide the necessary support throughout the pregnancy journey.

Physical and Emotional Changes in the Partner

Pregnancy brings about a series of profound physical and emotional changes. Understanding these changes can help you provide better support and empathy towards your partner during this transformative period.

Physical Changes

1. Hormonal Changes: Pregnancy significantly alters hormone levels, which affects almost every organ system in the body. Increased levels of hormones like progesterone and estrogen can cause a variety of symptoms.

2. Nausea and Morning Sickness: Common in the first trimester, these symptoms may extend into the second trimester for some women. Nausea is often triggered by certain odors, tastes, or even the stomach being too empty.

3. Weight Gain: A healthy pregnancy involves gradual weight gain. This is due to the growing baby, enlarged uterus, additional fat stores, increased blood volume, and other factors essential for supporting the pregnancy.

4. Changes in Appetite and Cravings: Many women experience changes in appetite and unusual food cravings or aversions, which can vary widely from one individual to another.

5. Increased Urination: The growing uterus puts pressure on the bladder, leading to increased frequency of urination throughout pregnancy.

6. Fatigue: Especially common in the first and third trimesters, fatigue results from hormonal changes, the physical demands of carrying extra weight, and later, the difficulty in finding a comfortable sleeping position.

7. Breast Changes: Breasts typically become larger, more tender, and sensitive as the body prepares for breastfeeding.

8. Skin Changes: Many women experience changes in skin tone, develop stretch marks, or notice increased acne and other skin changes due to hormonal influences.

9. Swelling: Fluid retention can lead to swelling in the feet, ankles, and hands, especially in the third trimester.

Emotional Changes

1. Mood Swings: Fluctuating hormone levels can cause significant mood changes. Feelings of joy can quickly turn into sadness or anxiety and vice versa.

2. Anxiety and Stress: Concerns about the health of the baby, the upcoming delivery, and changes in life roles can contribute to increased stress and anxiety.

3. Anticipatory Bonding: Many expectant mothers begin feeling a deepening bond with their baby, especially as they start to feel fetal movements.

4. Changes in Libido: Sexual desire may fluctuate due to physical discomfort, fatigue, or emotional reasons.

5. Concerns About Body Image: As the body changes, some women may feel self-conscious or unsure about their appearance.

How to Support Your Partner Through These Changes

1. Be Patient and Understanding: Acknowledge the physical and emotional changes your partner is experiencing. Offer reassurance, understanding, and patience.

2. Help with Daily Tasks: Taking on more household chores can alleviate physical and mental burdens, allowing your partner to rest and manage fatigue.

3. Communication: Keep communication lines open. Ask how your partner is feeling and what they need. Be a good listener and validate their experiences.

4. Encourage Healthy Habits: Support and participate in healthy lifestyle choices like balanced diets and moderate exercise. Help prepare nutritious meals.

5. Provide Emotional Support: Be there to comfort your partner during moments of anxiety or emotional distress. Small gestures of affection and attention can mean a lot.

6. Educate Yourself: The more you know about these changes and what to expect, the more effectively you can support your partner.

By understanding these changes and responding with empathy and support, you can help make the pregnancy experience a positive and memorable one for both of you.

Baby's Development Week by Week

Understanding the week-by-week development of your baby during pregnancy can be fascinating and help you feel more connected to the pregnancy. Here's a brief overview of key developmental milestones from conception to birth:

First Trimester

Weeks 1-2: Conception

- Pregnancy begins with the fertilization of an egg by a sperm, but for the first couple of weeks, your partner is not technically pregnant. The cycle prepares for pregnancy, and conception typically occurs about two weeks after the last menstrual period.

Week 3-4: Implantation

- The fertilized egg, now a blastocyst, implants itself in the wall of the uterus.
- The placenta and umbilical cord begin to form, which will nourish the baby throughout the pregnancy.

Week 5-6: Heartbeat

- The embryo's heart begins to form and beats at about twice the rate of an adult's.
- Basic facial features start to develop.

Week 7-8: Vital Organs

- The brain, lungs, and other vital organs start to form.
- The embryo begins to resemble a tiny human, with arm and leg buds visible.

Week 9-10: Bones and Cartilage

- Bones and cartilage begin to form.
- The baby's heart finishes dividing into four chambers, and the valves start to form.

Week 11-12: More Refined Features

- Fingers and toes lose their webbed appearance and become longer.
- External ears are fully formed, and the eyes are beginning to move closer together.

Second Trimester

Week 13-16: Rapid Growth

- The fetus undergoes a rapid growth spurt.

- Skin is still translucent, but hair, eyelashes, and eyebrows begin to grow.

Week 17-20: Movement

- You may begin to feel your baby's movements as they start to flex their arms and legs.
- The baby can hear muffled sounds from the outside world.

Week 21-24: Viability

- The baby's skin begins to produce vernix, a waxy coating that protects the skin from amniotic fluid.
- By around week 24, the baby has a chance of survival outside the womb, known as the age of viability.

Week 25-28: More Detail

- The baby's hair is now well-formed, and they start to add body fat.
- The lungs are developing rapidly, preparing for breathing outside the womb.

Third Trimester

Week 29-32: Increased Fat

- The baby continues to put on weight, mostly in the form of fat to regulate body temperature after birth.
- The bones are fully developed but still soft and pliable.

Week 33-36: Head Down

- The baby usually turns head down in preparation for birth.
- Sleeping patterns may become apparent, and you might notice periods of activity and rest.

Week 37-40: Full Term

- The baby is considered full term by week 37 and their organs are ready for life outside the womb.
- Breathing movements, sucking, and swallowing skills are well developed.

Week 41+: Overdue

- Some babies take a little longer! After week 40, doctors will monitor closely and may discuss inducing labor.

Each week of pregnancy brings new and exciting developments as your baby grows and prepares for birth. Being informed about these changes can enhance your connection to the pregnancy and prepare you for the arrival of your newborn.

Myths and Realities About Pregnancy

Pregnancy is a time filled with anticipation and curiosity, and also a time when many myths and misconceptions can circulate among family and friends. Understanding the realities behind these common myths can help you navigate pregnancy with better knowledge and less anxiety. Here are some prevalent myths about pregnancy, along with the realities:

Myth 1: Eating for Two

Reality: While it's true that nutrient needs increase during pregnancy, the idea of eating for two can be misleading. Pregnant women only need about 300 extra calories a day, especially in the second and third trimesters. Overeating can lead to excessive weight gain, which can pose risks like gestational diabetes and complications during delivery.

Myth 2: You Can't Exercise During Pregnancy

Reality: Exercise is not only safe but recommended during pregnancy unless there are specific medical conditions or complications. Moderate exercise, such as walking, swimming, and prenatal yoga, can help reduce pregnancy discomforts, improve sleep, increase energy levels, and prepare the body for childbirth. Always consult with a healthcare provider to tailor an exercise plan that's right for your pregnancy.

Myth 3: Avoid All Seafood

Reality: Not all seafood is off-limits during pregnancy. In fact, fish such as salmon, sardines, and trout are rich in omega-3 fatty acids, which are important for the baby's brain development. The key is to avoid fish with high levels of mercury, such as shark, swordfish, king mackerel, and tilefish. Pregnant women are advised to eat 8-12 ounces of low-mercury fish per week.

Myth 4: You Can't Have Coffee

Reality: Pregnant women don't have to give up caffeine entirely. The general guideline is to limit caffeine intake to less than 200 milligrams per day, which is about one 12-ounce cup of coffee. Excessive caffeine consumption has been linked to low birth weight and increased risk of miscarriage.

Myth 5: The Shape and Height of the Belly Can Predict the Baby's Gender

Reality: The shape and height of the belly are determined by factors such as the mother's body type, the baby's position, and muscle tone, not the baby's gender. Ultrasounds and other medical tests are the only reliable ways to determine the gender of the baby.

Myth 6: Don't Fly During Pregnancy

Reality: Flying is generally safe for pregnant women until about 36 weeks, as long as there are no pregnancy complications or risks of preterm labor. It's important to walk around every couple of hours to reduce the risk of blood clots and stay hydrated during the flight.

Myth 7: No Hair Dying or Nails Painting

Reality: Most research indicates that it's generally safe to color your hair or use nail polish during pregnancy, especially after the first trimester. However, it's recommended to use products with less harsh chemicals and ensure good ventilation during application to avoid inhaling fumes.

Myth 8: Full Moon Can Trigger Labor

Reality: No scientific studies have confirmed that the lunar cycle can influence the timing of labor. Labor onset is more likely influenced by physiological changes in the mother's body rather than environmental factors like the lunar phase.

Myth 9: You Shouldn't Have Cats Around During Pregnancy

Reality: Cats themselves are not a risk to a pregnancy, but pregnant women should avoid handling cat litter, which can carry toxoplasmosis, a rare infection that could potentially harm the baby. It's safe to be around cats, but it's best to have someone else handle the litter box.

By dispelling these myths with factual information, you can help create a healthier, more informed pregnancy experience. If you're ever in doubt, it's always best to consult with your healthcare provider.

3. Preparing for Fatherhood
Common Expectations and Fears

During pregnancy, both expectant mothers and fathers often have a mixture of expectations and fears. Understanding these common feelings can help couples address concerns proactively and provide reassurance. Here's an overview of some typical expectations and fears that new parents might experience:

Common Expectations

1. **Joy and Excitement**: Many expectant parents envision the joy of holding their newborn, imagining the first moments of bonding and the deep connection they will feel.
2. **Planning the Future**: Parents often enjoy planning for the future, from decorating the nursery to imagining their child's life milestones like first steps and first words.
3. **Stronger Relationship Bonds**: There's an expectation that having a baby will bring the couple closer together, strengthening their bond through shared responsibility and love for their child.
4. **Parental Instincts**: Many expect that parental instincts will naturally kick in, guiding them intuitively on how to care for their baby.

Common Fears

1. **Health Concerns**: Both mothers and fathers commonly worry about the health of the baby and the mother during pregnancy and childbirth. Fears about complications during delivery or health issues for the baby can be prominent.
2. **Financial Pressure**: The costs associated with raising a child can be daunting. Many expectant parents worry about providing financially for their family, covering everything from medical bills to education costs.
3. **Change in Lifestyle**: The transition to parenthood often brings a fear of losing personal freedom or the ability to pursue personal interests. Parents may worry about the loss of spontaneity in their lives or the ability to travel and socialize.
4. **Impact on the Relationship**: Some couples fear that the arrival of a baby might negatively affect their relationship, particularly if they've heard stories of stress and sleep deprivation putting a strain on intimacy and partnership.
5. **Parenting Skills**: Doubts about one's ability to be a good parent are common. Many worry if they will know how to handle a baby, manage crying, or cope with the day-to-day responsibilities of parenting.
6. **Body Image**: Particularly for mothers, changes in body shape and weight can lead to anxiety and concerns about physical appearance and self-esteem.

How to Address These Expectations and Fears

Open Communication: Regular, open discussions about each other's feelings, hopes, and worries can help alleviate anxiety. It's important for partners to listen to each other without judgment and offer support.

Education and Preparation: Attending prenatal classes together, reading about pregnancy and child care, and talking to experienced parents can demystify aspects of childbirth and parenting, reducing fear of the unknown.

Financial Planning: Setting up a financial plan that covers prenatal care, childbirth, and future child-rearing expenses can reduce anxiety related to financial pressures.

Relationship Nurturing: It's vital to keep the relationship a priority, setting aside time for each other and maintaining intimacy to strengthen the bond before the baby arrives.

Seek Professional Help: If fears and anxiety become overwhelming, it might be helpful to talk to a counselor or therapist who specializes in prenatal and postpartum issues.

Understanding these common expectations and fears allows couples to better prepare for the challenges and rewards of parenthood, fostering a supportive environment for each other during this transformative time.

Your Mindset: How to Prepare Psychologically

Preparing psychologically for parenthood is crucial for both expectant mothers and fathers. Parenthood brings significant changes, and having a healthy mindset can greatly impact your experience positively. Here are some strategies to prepare yourself mentally for the journey ahead:

Understanding the Changes

Acknowledge the Transition: Recognize that life will change in various ways, including your routines, priorities, and relationships. Accepting that these changes are part of becoming a parent can help you adapt more readily.

Educate Yourself: Knowledge is power. The more you know about pregnancy, childbirth, and parenting, the more confident you'll feel. Read books, attend classes, and seek advice from trusted sources to build your understanding and skills.

Building Emotional Resilience

Develop Coping Strategies: Parenthood can be stressful. Identify stress-relief techniques that work for you, such as exercise, meditation, journaling, or talking things out with friends or a partner. These can be vital tools when faced with parenting challenges.

Focus on the Positive: While it's important to be realistic about the challenges of parenting, focusing on the positive aspects can boost your mood and outlook. Think about the joys and rewards that come with raising a child.

Strengthening Relationships

Communicate Openly with Your Partner: Parenthood can strain relationships. Strengthen your relationship by discussing expectations, fears, and how you plan to support each other. Make a habit of checking in regularly on each other's feelings and needs.

Build a Support Network: Connect with other parents or parenting groups. Having a community can provide emotional support and practical advice. They can also offer a sense of camaraderie and understanding.

Practicing Flexibility

Adaptability Is Key: Not everything will go as planned. Being flexible and able to adjust your expectations can reduce frustration and anxiety. This flexibility will be invaluable during labor, childbirth, and the early days of parenting.

Preparing Mentally for Labor and Delivery

Understand the Process: Familiarize yourself with the stages of labor and delivery options. Knowing what to expect can reduce fear and anxiety.

Develop a Birth Plan: While it's essential to remain flexible, having a birth plan can give you a sense of control and peace of mind. Discuss this plan with your partner and healthcare provider, and be prepared to adapt if necessary.

Embracing the Role

Visualize Your Role as a Parent: Spend time thinking about the kind of parent you want to be. Visualization can be a powerful tool for mentally preparing for a new role.

Stay Involved: For expectant fathers, staying involved during the pregnancy can help you bond with your baby and partner. Attend prenatal visits and ultrasounds, help with nursery preparations, and be active in learning about the baby's development.

Taking Care of Your Mental Health

Monitor Your Mental Health: Pay attention to signs of excessive stress or depression. It's important to seek help early if you feel overwhelmed or unable to cope.

Self-care: Prioritize your own health and well-being. Good physical health supports mental health, so maintain a healthy diet, get regular exercise, and ensure you're getting enough sleep.

Preparing psychologically for parenthood means setting realistic expectations, strengthening your support systems, and developing resilience. By taking these steps, you can ensure that you are mentally ready to embrace the challenges and joys of becoming a parent.

Communicating with Your Partner: Listening and Support

Effective communication with your partner is crucial during pregnancy, as it strengthens your relationship and ensures both of you feel supported and connected. Here are practical tips on how to enhance communication, focusing on listening and providing support:

Active Listening

Give Full Attention: When your partner is speaking, give them your undivided attention. Put away distractions like phones or tablets, make eye contact, and show that you are engaged.

Encourage Expression: Encourage your partner to express their thoughts and feelings fully. Sometimes, they might need to vent or share concerns without immediately looking for solutions.

Validate Feelings: Acknowledge your partner's feelings without judgment. Saying things like "It makes sense you feel that way," or "I can see why that's upsetting," helps validate their emotions and shows empathy.

Reflect Back: Paraphrase or summarize what your partner has said to ensure you understand correctly. For example, "It sounds like you're feeling overwhelmed with the nursery preparations, is that right?"

Expressive Communication

Share Your Own Feelings: Open up about your own emotions and experiences. Sharing can build intimacy and trust, showing your partner that it's safe to express vulnerabilities.

Be Clear and Direct: Be honest and clear about your own needs and expectations. Misunderstandings often arise from assumptions or indirect communication.

Use "I" Statements: When discussing issues, use "I" statements instead of "you" statements to avoid sounding accusatory. For example, say, "I feel worried when I don't know the doctor's appointment details," instead of, "You never tell me what's happening with the appointments."

Providing Support

Ask What They Need: Instead of assuming what your partner needs, directly ask them how you can support them. Their needs can change, and what worked before might not be helpful now.

Offer Practical Help: Take on tasks that can ease your partner's burden, such as running errands, cooking meals, or doing extra chores around the house.

Plan Together: Involve each other in decisions and planning, from things like preparing the baby's room to financial planning. Shared responsibilities strengthen partnership.

Handling Disagreements

Stay Respectful: Keep discussions respectful, even when you disagree. Avoid raising your voice or using harsh words.

Take Breaks if Needed: If a conversation gets too heated, it's okay to take a break and revisit the discussion when both partners are calmer.

Seek to Resolve: Always aim for resolution or compromise. Understand that compromise doesn't mean one person gives in completely, but rather that both find a solution that works for both.

Building Emotional Intimacy

Regular Check-ins: Establish regular times to check in with each other about your day, feelings, and any upcoming concerns. This can prevent issues from building up.

Celebrate Together: Share excitement and positive anticipation about the changes and the future. Celebrate milestones in the pregnancy together to reinforce a positive bond.

Practice Appreciation: Regularly express appreciation for each other's efforts and qualities. Feeling appreciated can significantly enhance emotional connection and satisfaction in the relationship.

By prioritizing effective communication, listening actively, and providing emotional and practical support, you can strengthen your relationship and navigate the journey of pregnancy together as a cohesive and supportive team.

Couple Exercise #1 : Create a List of Expectations and Fears

Creating a list of expectations and fears together as a couple is a powerful exercise that can enhance communication, deepen understanding, and help both partners feel more connected and prepared for the changes that come with pregnancy and parenthood. Here's a step-by-step guide on how to conduct this exercise effectively:

Step 1: Set a Comfortable and Distraction-Free Environment

Choose a quiet, comfortable setting where you both feel relaxed and free from interruptions. Ensure you have enough time to discuss without feeling rushed. Maybe make some tea or coffee, and sit together in a cozy space.

Step 2: Prepare for Open Sharing

Start the exercise by affirming the importance of open, honest, and non-judgmental communication. Emphasize that this is a safe space to share feelings, hopes, and worries.

Step 3: Brainstorming Session

Each partner takes some time to individually write down their own expectations and fears related to the pregnancy, birth, and early parenting stages. Consider different aspects such as emotional changes, physical changes, lifestyle adjustments, financial implications, and your relationship dynamics.

Step 4: Share and Discuss

Take turns sharing your lists with each other. As one partner shares, the other should listen actively, without interrupting or offering solutions immediately. Use active listening techniques such as nodding, maintaining eye contact, and using encouraging phrases like "tell me more" or "how does that make you feel?"

Step 5: Validate Each Other's Feelings

After each partner has shared, take a moment to acknowledge and validate each other's feelings. It's important to recognize that fears and expectations are both valid and significant. This helps to foster empathy and support between partners.

Step 6: Identify Common Themes

Look for common themes or areas where your expectations and fears overlap. This can help you identify shared concerns or hopes that you might address or celebrate together.

Step 7: Develop Action Plans

For each common fear or significant expectation, discuss possible ways to address or prepare for these aspects. For example, if both partners are worried about finances, you might plan to consult a financial advisor or set up a new savings plan. If there are fears about the birth itself, consider enrolling together in childbirth education classes.

Step 8: Commit to Ongoing Communication

Acknowledge that feelings and situations can change, and commit to revisiting this conversation regularly. You might set a monthly "check-in" where you update your feelings, discuss new fears or expectations, and adjust your plans accordingly.

Step 9: Create a Supportive Atmosphere

End the exercise by expressing appreciation for each other's openness and support. Continue to encourage each other and maintain a supportive environment as you navigate pregnancy and parenthood together.

Step 10: Optional Follow-Up with a Professional

If during the exercise, significant issues arise that seem difficult to manage, consider following up with a counselor or therapist who specializes in prenatal and family issues. They can offer professional guidance and additional strategies to support you both.

This exercise not only promotes better mutual understanding but also strengthens your partnership by aligning your expectations and preparing jointly for upcoming changes, creating a unified approach to tackling the challenges and joys of becoming parents.

4. Health and Wellness

Importance of Physical and Mental Health for Both

Maintaining both physical and mental health during pregnancy is essential not only for the expectant mother but also for the partner. Healthy parents are more likely to have a healthy pregnancy and baby, and they are better equipped to handle the demands of new parenthood. Here's why it's crucial for both partners to focus on their physical and mental well-being:

Importance of Physical Health

1. Better Pregnancy Outcomes: For the expectant mother, good physical health can reduce the risk of pregnancy complications such as gestational diabetes and preeclampsia. It can also influence the health of the baby, affecting birth weight and reducing the risk of future chronic conditions.

2. Increased Energy Levels: Pregnancy and the postpartum period can be physically demanding. Maintaining fitness can help both partners feel more energetic and capable of managing the sleep deprivation and physical demands of caring for a newborn.

3. Easier Labor and Recovery: For the birthing mother, regular exercise and a healthy body can lead to an easier labor and quicker recovery post-birth. Strong muscles and good stamina can be beneficial during childbirth.

4. Reducing Discomfort: Exercise and a healthy diet can help mitigate common pregnancy discomforts like back pain, bloating, and constipation. It also helps maintain a healthy weight, which can reduce physical discomforts associated with being overweight or underweight.

Importance of Mental Health

1. Emotional Resilience: The ability to handle stress, anxiety, and the emotional highs and lows of pregnancy and new parenthood is bolstered by good mental health. This resilience is crucial for both parents as they navigate the challenges of this life-changing period.

2. Bonding with the Baby: Good mental health supports positive interactions between the parents and the baby. A mentally healthy parent is more likely to be responsive and sensitive to the baby's needs, which is crucial for the child's emotional and social development.

3. Reducing the Risk of Postpartum Depression: Both mothers and fathers can experience postpartum depression or anxiety. Maintaining mental health during the pregnancy can reduce the risk and severity of postpartum mood disorders.

4. Relationship Health: Mental health challenges can strain relationships. Couples who manage their mental health well tend to have stronger, more supportive relationships, which is vital when adjusting to life with a new baby.

Strategies to Maintain Physical and Mental Health

1. Regular Exercise: Engage in moderate exercise like walking, prenatal yoga, or swimming. These activities are excellent for fitness and can also be a great stress reliever.

2. Balanced Diet: Eat a balanced diet rich in vitamins, minerals, and essential nutrients that support the health of both mother and baby. Avoid excessive caffeine and junk food, which can negatively impact both physical and mental health.

3. Adequate Rest: Ensure both partners get enough sleep. While this can be challenging, prioritize rest and develop a sleep routine to help manage sleep deprivation.

4. Stress Management: Use relaxation techniques such as deep breathing, meditation, or mindfulness. These practices can help manage stress levels and improve overall mental health.

5. Seek Support: Don't hesitate to seek support from healthcare providers, counselors, or support groups if you are struggling with physical or mental health issues. Professional help can provide effective strategies and support systems to manage health during and after pregnancy.

6. Open Communication: Maintain open lines of communication with your partner about how you're feeling physically and emotionally. Sharing your experiences and challenges can help both partners feel understood and supported.

By taking proactive steps to maintain physical and mental health, expectant parents can better enjoy the pregnancy journey, prepare for a healthy delivery, and set the foundation for a rewarding experience with their new baby.

Healthy Eating During Pregnancy

Eating a balanced and nutritious diet during pregnancy is crucial for the health of both the mother and the baby. It supports the baby's growth and development and helps the mother manage the physical demands of pregnancy and prepare for breastfeeding. Here's a guide to healthy eating during pregnancy:

Key Nutrients

1. Folic Acid (Folate):

- **Importance:** Helps prevent neural tube defects, such as spina bifida.
- **Sources:** Leafy greens, fortified cereals, legumes, and citrus fruits.

2. Iron:

- **Importance:** Supports the development of the placenta and fetus and helps prevent anemia.
- **Sources:** Red meat, poultry, fish, lentils, spinach, and iron-fortified cereals.

3. Calcium:

- **Importance:** Essential for building the baby's bones and teeth.
- **Sources:** Dairy products, broccoli, kale, and fortified plant-based beverages.

4. Vitamin D:

- **Importance:** Works with calcium to help the baby's bones and teeth develop.
- **Sources:** Fortified dairy and plant-based milks, fatty fish, and sunlight.

5. Omega-3 Fatty Acids:

- **Importance:** Important for brain development.
- **Sources:** Fish like salmon and sardines, flaxseeds, walnuts, and chia seeds.

6. Protein:

- **Importance:** Crucial for the growth of fetal tissue, including the brain, and helps breast and uterine tissue to grow during pregnancy.
- **Sources:** Lean meat, poultry, fish, eggs, beans, tofu, and nuts.

Eating Strategies

1. Small, Frequent Meals:

- Eating smaller, more frequent meals can help manage nausea, maintain steady blood sugar levels, and manage heartburn, which is common as pregnancy progresses.

2. Stay Hydrated:

- Drinking plenty of fluids is important to support all of your body's functions. Aim for about 10 cups (2.3 liters) of fluids a day, which can include water, milk, and small amounts of juice.

3. Limit Certain Foods:

- **Raw or Undercooked Foods:** Avoid raw fish, meats, or eggs due to the risk of contamination with bacteria or parasites.
- **High-Mercury Fish:** Avoid shark, swordfish, king mackerel, and tilefish due to high levels of mercury.
- **Unpasteurized Foods:** Stay away from unpasteurized milk, cheese, and fruit juices, as they can harbor harmful bacteria.

4. Manage Caffeine Intake:

- Limit caffeine to less than 200 mg per day, equivalent to about one 12-ounce cup of coffee.

5. Avoid Alcohol:

- No amount of alcohol is considered safe during pregnancy, as it can lead to fetal alcohol spectrum disorders.

Tips for Nutritional Success

1. Plan Your Meals:

- Planning helps ensure you get a balanced intake of nutrients. Consider preparing meals in advance to help with managing fatigue and busy schedules.

2. Listen to Your Body:

- Your body will often signal what it needs. If you're craving certain foods, it might be your body's way of pointing to nutritional needs, though cravings should be indulged in moderation.

3. Consult a Nutritionist:

- If you have specific dietary needs or restrictions, consulting with a dietitian or nutritionist can help ensure you're getting all the necessary nutrients.

4. Prenatal Vitamins:

- Prenatal vitamins can complement your diet, ensuring you get enough essential nutrients like folic acid and iron. These should be taken under the guidance of your healthcare provider.

Healthy eating during pregnancy doesn't just support the physical development of the baby; it also impacts the mother's energy levels and overall well-being. By focusing on a balanced diet rich in essential nutrients, expectant mothers can better handle the demands of pregnancy and prepare for a healthy delivery.

Physical Activity: What to Do and What to Avoid

Physical activity during pregnancy can offer numerous benefits for both the mother and the baby, including improved mood, better sleep, reduced risk of excessive weight gain, and easier labor. However, it's also important to know which types of activities are safe and which should be avoided. Here's a guide to help you navigate physical activity during pregnancy:

Recommended Physical Activities

1. Walking:

- One of the safest and most effective forms of exercise for pregnant women. It doesn't require any special equipment and can be easily adjusted to your fitness level.

2. Prenatal Yoga:

- Focuses on gentle stretching and is designed to enhance flexibility, mental centering, and breathing. Prenatal yoga can help relieve tension and maintain muscle tone.

3. Swimming and Water Aerobics:

- Swimming is excellent for pregnant women because the water supports your weight, reducing the strain on your back and joints. It also provides a good cardiovascular workout.

4. Stationary Cycling:

- A safe way to raise your heart rate without the risk of falling. As your belly grows, maintaining balance becomes more challenging, making stationary cycling a preferable option.

5. Low-Impact Aerobics:

- Classes designed for pregnant women focus on limiting jumps and high impacts. These classes promote heart health and muscle tone without excessive strain.

6. Strength Training:

- Can be continued during pregnancy but with modifications to accommodate changes in balance and strength. Focus on lighter weights and avoid lying flat on your back, especially after the first trimester.

Activities to Avoid

1. Contact Sports:

- Sports like soccer, basketball, and hockey come with a high risk of injury and should be avoided during pregnancy.

2. Activities with a High Risk of Falling:

- Skiing, horseback riding, and off-road cycling can increase the risk of injury to yourself and your baby and should be avoided.

3. Scuba Diving:

- As you ascend, air bubbles can form in your bloodstream, which can be dangerous for both you and your developing baby.

4. High-Altitude Exercise:

- Exercising above 6,000 feet can put you at risk for altitude sickness and should be avoided unless you are already acclimated to high altitudes before pregnancy.

5. Lying Flat on Your Back:

- After the first trimester, lying flat on your back can cause the weight of the uterus to press on the vein that returns blood from your lower body to your heart. This can decrease blood flow and lead to dizziness, shortness of breath, or other issues.

6. Hot Yoga or Hot Pilates:

- High temperatures in these classes can raise your body temperature to levels that are unsafe during pregnancy.

Tips for Safe Exercise During Pregnancy

1. Always Warm Up and Cool Down:

- Proper warm-ups and cool-downs are crucial to prevent muscle strain and increase comfort during exercise.

2. Listen to Your Body:

- Pay attention to what your body is telling you. If you feel pain or discomfort, stop and rest. If symptoms persist, consult your healthcare provider.

3. Stay Hydrated:

- Drink plenty of water before, during, and after exercise to avoid dehydration, which can increase the risk of overheating and even trigger contractions.

4. Wear Appropriate Clothing:

- Comfortable, non-restrictive clothing and a supportive bra can make exercise more comfortable.

5. Monitor Your Heart Rate:

- Keeping your heart rate at a moderate level ensures safety for you and the baby. The "talk test" (being able to hold a conversation while exercising) is a useful way to monitor the intensity.

6. Consult Your Healthcare Provider:

- Before starting any exercise program, it's important to discuss it with your healthcare provider to ensure it's safe for your specific pregnancy conditions.

Incorporating regular, appropriate physical activity into your daily routine can significantly benefit your pregnancy experience and potentially lead to a smoother labor and recovery process.

How to Reduce Stress for You and Your Partner

Reducing stress during pregnancy is essential for both the health of the expectant mother and the baby. High levels of stress can have various negative impacts, including affecting the baby's development. Here are practical strategies to help both you and your partner manage stress effectively during this transformative time:

Regular Exercise

Physical activity is a proven stress reliever. Encourage each other to engage in safe pregnancy exercises like walking, prenatal yoga, or swimming. Regular exercise can improve overall health, boost mood through the release of endorphins, and help manage sleep issues.

Adequate Rest and Sleep

Sleep is crucial for stress reduction. Help create a relaxing bedtime routine and make the sleeping environment comfortable. Consider using extra pillows for support, limiting screen time before bed, and establishing a consistent sleep schedule.

Healthy Eating

A well-balanced diet supports physical health, which can help manage stress levels. Include plenty of fruits, vegetables, whole grains, and lean proteins in your daily meals. Avoid high-sugar and high-fat foods that can lead to energy crashes and mood swings.

Mindfulness and Relaxation Techniques

Practices such as deep breathing exercises, meditation, or prenatal yoga can help both partners stay calm and grounded. These techniques can be particularly helpful during moments of high stress or anxiety.

Open Communication

Keep the lines of communication open. Regularly talk about your feelings, fears, and expectations with each other. Being able to share and listen can significantly reduce stress and build a stronger, more supportive relationship.

Time Management

Avoid the stress of feeling rushed or overwhelmed by managing your time effectively. Prioritize tasks, delegate responsibilities, and don't hesitate to say no to unnecessary commitments. Planning and organization can prevent last-minute pressures.

Couple Time

Maintain your relationship by scheduling regular date nights or special moments together. Keeping your emotional connection strong can provide a great source of comfort and stability for both of you.

Support Network

Lean on friends, family, or support groups who can offer advice, help, or just an understanding ear. Knowing you have a reliable support system can alleviate the feeling of having to manage everything on your own.

Professional Help

If stress becomes overwhelming, consider seeking help from a professional counselor or therapist. They can provide strategies to manage stress effectively and help navigate any relationship challenges that arise during pregnancy.

Prenatal Classes

Attend prenatal classes together. These classes not only educate you about the pregnancy and childbirth process but also provide an opportunity to meet other expectant parents who can relate to your experiences.

Hobbies and Leisure Activities

Encourage each other to engage in activities you find relaxing and enjoyable. Whether it's reading, crafting, gardening, or watching movies, spending time on leisure activities can provide a necessary break from the routine and help manage stress.

By integrating these strategies into your daily lives, both you and your partner can help ensure a healthier, less stressful pregnancy experience. Remember, taking care of your mental health is just as important as monitoring physical health during this significant period.

Couple Exercise #2: Prepare Healthy Meals Together

Preparing healthy meals together is not only a practical way to ensure good nutrition during pregnancy, but it's also a wonderful opportunity to bond and share responsibilities. Here's a guide on how to make the most out of cooking together as a couple, including tips on meal planning, preparation, and making the experience enjoyable and stress-free.

Step 1: Plan Your Meals Together

Collaborate on Menu Planning:

- Sit down together once a week to plan your meals. Consider nutritional needs specific to pregnancy, like incorporating foods rich in folic acid, iron, calcium, and fiber.
- Choose recipes that are balanced and include a variety of food groups.

Create a Grocery List:

- Make a shopping list based on your meal plan. Divide the list into categories to make shopping more efficient and ensure you don't forget any ingredients.

Step 2: Shop Together

Make Shopping a Joint Effort:

- If possible, go grocery shopping together. This can help make decisions on food choices and substitutions easier and ensures both partners' preferences are considered.

Step 3: Prepare the Cooking Space

Organize the Kitchen:

- Clear and clean your cooking space before you start. An organized kitchen can make the cooking process smoother and more enjoyable.
- Gather all necessary utensils and ingredients before starting to avoid mid-recipe disruptions.

Step 4: Cook Together

Assign Tasks:

- Divide the cooking tasks according to each partner's comfort and skill level. One can handle chopping and prep work, while the other manages the cooking.
- Switch roles occasionally to learn new skills and keep the activity engaging.

Experiment and Learn Together:

- Try new recipes and cooking techniques together. Cooking classes, online tutorials, **and cookbooks can be great resources for learning and trying out new ideas.**

Step 5: Focus on Hygiene and Safety

Practice Good Food Safety:

- Be mindful of food safety, especially important during pregnancy. Wash hands and surfaces often, keep raw meats separate from other foods, cook to safe temperatures, and refrigerate promptly.

Step 6: Make It Fun

Enjoy the Process:

- Play your favorite music, chat about your day, or share stories as you cook. The goal is to make meal preparation a relaxing and enjoyable time together.
- Treat cooking as a date activity. Light candles, set the table nicely, and perhaps dress up a bit to celebrate your effort once the meal is ready.

Step 7: Sit Down and Enjoy

Eat Together:

- Always sit down to eat together without distractions like TV or smartphones. This is a time to enjoy the food you've made and spend quality time together.
- Discuss the meal—what you liked, what you might change for next time, and appreciate each other's efforts.

Step 8: Clean Up Together

Share the Cleanup Duties:

- After the meal, clear and clean the kitchen together. Sharing the cleanup makes the task lighter and faster, and it's a continuation of your teamwork.

Step 9: Reflect and Adjust

Review and Improve:

- Regularly discuss what works and what doesn't in your cooking routine. Make adjustments to recipes, the cooking process, or meal planning as needed.

This couple's activity not only promotes healthy eating habits but also strengthens the relationship by building teamwork, communication, and sharing the joys (and sometimes the disasters) of cooking together.

5. Medical Visits and Tests
Overview of Prenatal Visits

Prenatal visits are crucial for monitoring the health of both the mother and the baby throughout the pregnancy. These appointments allow healthcare providers to track the baby's growth, assess the mother's health, and address any concerns that might arise. Here's a general overview of what to expect during these visits:

First Trimester

Initial Appointment (Usually around 6-8 weeks):

- **Medical History:** Your healthcare provider will take a comprehensive medical history of both parents.
- **Physical Exam:** This includes a pelvic exam, Pap smear (if due), and possibly a breast exam.
- **Blood Tests:** Common tests include blood type, Rh factor, and a complete blood count (CBC). Tests for immunity to certain diseases and sexually transmitted infections (STIs) may also be performed.
- **Urine Tests:** Urine is checked for infections and glucose levels.
- **Ultrasound:** An early ultrasound may be conducted to confirm the pregnancy and estimate the due date.
- **Counseling:** Discussion about lifestyle, nutrition, prenatal vitamins, and what to expect in the coming months.

Second Trimester

Follow-Up Visits (Every 4 weeks):

- **Checkups:** Monitoring blood pressure, weight, and urine.
- **Ultrasound (around 18-22 weeks):** This detailed scan checks the baby's anatomy, the placenta's position, and amniotic fluid levels.
- **Glucose Screening Test (around 24-28 weeks):** To check for gestational diabetes.
- **Blood Tests:** Might include checking iron levels to screen for anemia.
- **Fetal Heart Rate Monitoring:** Listening to the baby's heartbeat.

Third Trimester

Follow-Up Visits (Every 2-3 weeks, then weekly after 36 weeks):

- **Physical Exams:** Continue to monitor weight, blood pressure, and urine.

- **Fetal Monitoring:** Checking baby's growth, position, and movements.
- **Group B Strep Test (around 35-37 weeks):** To check for the presence of Group B streptococcus, which can be harmful to the baby during delivery.
- **Discussion of Labor and Delivery Plans:** Topics might include pain relief options, what to bring to the hospital, and signs of labor.
- **Pelvic Exams:** In the final weeks, to check for changes in the cervix that indicate preparation for childbirth.

Additional Considerations

High-Risk Pregnancies:

- More frequent visits and specialized tests might be required if the pregnancy is considered high-risk due to factors like advanced maternal age, twins or multiple pregnancies, or pre-existing medical conditions.

Questions and Concerns:

- Prenatal visits are a great opportunity to address any questions or concerns about pregnancy, labor, delivery, or postpartum issues. It's helpful to come prepared with a list of questions to each appointment.

Support:

- Partners are encouraged to attend prenatal appointments whenever possible. This can help them stay informed and involved in the pregnancy journey.

Regular prenatal care is essential for ensuring the health and safety of both the mother and the baby. It provides critical medical support and fosters a positive, informative relationship with healthcare providers throughout the pregnancy.

Common Tests and Screenings During Pregnancy

During pregnancy, a variety of tests and screenings are performed to monitor the health of both the mother and the baby, and to identify any potential health issues early on. Here's a rundown of common tests and screenings you can expect during pregnancy:

First Trimester

1. Blood Tests:

- **Complete Blood Count (CBC):** To check for anemia or other blood disorders.
- **Blood Type and Rh Factor:** To determine blood type and Rh factor compatibility issues.

- **Rubella Immunity:** To ensure immunity against rubella, which can harm the developing baby.
- **Hepatitis B, HIV, and Syphilis Screening:** Important for the health of both mother and baby.

2. Urine Tests:

- Routinely performed to check for urinary tract infections, proteinuria (protein in the urine), and glycosuria (sugar in the urine), which can indicate diabetes.

3. Ultrasound:

- **Dating Ultrasound:** Performed to confirm the due date, check for a fetal heartbeat, and rule out ectopic pregnancies.

4. Chorionic Villus Sampling (CVS):

- **Optional:** Typically offered to women at higher risk of chromosomal or genetic disorders. CVS can be performed between 10 and 13 weeks to detect conditions like Down syndrome and other genetic disorders.

Second Trimester

1. Ultrasound:

- **Anatomy Scan (around 18-22 weeks):** This detailed ultrasound checks the baby's overall development, including the brain, heart, kidneys, limbs, and other vital organs. It also checks the placenta's position and amniotic fluid levels.

2. Quadruple Screen:

- **Optional:** A blood test that assesses the likelihood of certain genetic disorders and neural tube defects. It measures levels of AFP, hCG, Estriol, and Inhibin A.

3. Glucose Screening Test:

- Performed between 24-28 weeks to check for gestational diabetes by assessing how well the body processes sugar.

Third Trimester

1. Group B Streptococcus (GBS) Screening:

- Typically done between 35-37 weeks. GBS is a common bacterium that can be harmless in adults but can pose serious health risks to newborns if transmitted during childbirth.

2. Repeat Blood Tests:

- If needed, repeat tests for conditions like anemia or Rh incompatibility may be conducted.

3. Biophysical Profile:

- **Optional:** This test may be recommended in high-risk pregnancies or if there are concerns about the baby's health. It combines an ultrasound with a non-stress test to assess the baby's movement, heart rate, breathing, and amniotic fluid level.

4. Non-Stress Test:

- **Optional:** Usually recommended if there are concerns about the baby's activity or in pregnancies that go beyond the due date. It monitors fetal heart rate and response to movement.

Importance of Regular Prenatal Visits

Regular prenatal visits are crucial to ensure these tests are performed at appropriate times. They provide opportunities to catch potential issues early and manage them effectively. Always discuss any concerns about tests or your pregnancy in general with your healthcare provider, who can offer detailed explanations and guidance based on your specific health needs.

How to Actively Participate in Medical Visits

Actively participating in medical visits during pregnancy can significantly enhance the care you receive, making the experience more beneficial and reassuring for both you and your partner. Here are practical tips on how to be more engaged during prenatal appointments:

Prepare for Appointments

1. Write Down Questions and Concerns: Before each visit, take some time to jot down any questions or concerns you have. This could include queries about symptoms, the baby's development, the progress of your pregnancy, lifestyle adjustments, or the birth plan. Having a list will ensure you don't forget to ask important questions.

2. Review Previous Advice: Look over the notes from your last visit to see if there are follow-up questions or issues that need readdressing. This helps keep your care continuous and informed.

During the Visit

3. Bring a Partner or Support Person: If possible, bring your partner or a support person to the appointments. They can help remember information, provide emotional support, and ask questions you might not think of.

4. Take Notes: Write down important points your healthcare provider makes or consider recording the conversation (with permission). This can help you remember advice and instructions given during the appointment.

5. Discuss Your Symptoms and Changes: Be open about any new symptoms or changes you've noticed, no matter how small they may seem. Information that you provide can be crucial in monitoring the health of both you and your baby.

6. Clarify Your Understanding: If your healthcare provider gives you new information or instructions, repeat them back in your own words to confirm your understanding. Don't hesitate to ask for clarification if something isn't clear.

Ask Proactive Questions

7. Inquire About Tests and Procedures: When a test or procedure is recommended, ask what it's for, what it entails, possible risks, and how you should prepare. Knowing the purpose and what to expect can reduce anxiety and make the process smoother.

8. Discuss the Birth Plan: As your due date approaches, discuss your birth plan and preferences. Ask about pain relief options, labor and delivery processes, and what to expect at the hospital or birthing center.

9. Request Resources: Ask for recommendations on books, classes, or online resources where you can learn more about pregnancy, childbirth, and parenting.

Follow Up

10. Review and Follow Instructions: Review any instructions or guidance provided by your healthcare provider before leaving. Make sure you understand any medication prescriptions, dietary recommendations, or restrictions advised during the visit.

11. Schedule Next Appointment: Before leaving the office, schedule your next appointment. Keeping track of your appointment schedule helps maintain regular monitoring and care throughout the pregnancy.

12. Contact for Concerns: Ensure you know how to contact your healthcare provider if any issues or questions arise before your next scheduled visit. Knowing whom to call and how to reach them can provide reassurance and quick access to advice when needed.

Active participation in prenatal visits empowers you to take charge of your health and that of your baby. It builds a partnership with your healthcare provider, ensuring that your needs and concerns are addressed, and ultimately contributes to a healthier pregnancy and delivery experience.

Useful Questions to Ask the Doctor

When attending prenatal appointments, having a set of prepared questions can help you gain a clearer understanding of your pregnancy and what to expect. Here are some useful questions to consider asking your doctor during your prenatal visits:

General Health and Pregnancy Management

1. How is my due date calculated, and can it change based on ultrasound results?
2. What are the normal symptoms I should expect throughout my pregnancy?
3. Are there specific symptoms that should prompt me to call you or go to the hospital?
4. What prenatal vitamins do you recommend, and why?
5. Can you recommend a balanced diet plan during my pregnancy?
6. How much weight gain is healthy for me during my pregnancy?
7. What level and type of exercise is safe for me throughout my pregnancy?

Tests and Screenings

8. What routine tests and screenings do you recommend, and what are their purposes?
9. Are there any optional tests I should consider, such as genetic screening?
10. What do my ultrasound scans tell us about the baby's health and development?
11. Are there any specific concerns or things to look for in the test results?

Lifestyle Concerns

12. What lifestyle changes should I consider to support a healthy pregnancy (e.g., travel, pets, hobbies)?
13. Are there any restrictions on sexual activity during pregnancy?
14. Can I continue to work throughout my pregnancy? Are there modifications I should make to my work routine?

Managing Health Issues

15. How can we manage existing health issues, like diabetes or hypertension, during pregnancy?
16. What should I do if I catch a cold or flu? Are over-the-counter medications safe during pregnancy?
17. What are the signs of gestational diabetes or preeclampsia, and how would they be managed if diagnosed?

Birth Planning

18. What are the signs of labor I should watch for?
19. When should I come to the hospital after labor begins?

20. Can we discuss my birth plan in detail? What are your policies on pain relief during labor?
21. What are the policies regarding support people in the delivery room?
22. In case of a C-section, what would be the procedure and recovery like?

Postpartum Care

23. What should I expect during the postpartum period?
24. How soon after delivery should I schedule a postpartum visit?
25. What are the common signs of postpartum depression, and where can I get help if I need it?
26. What advice do you have about breastfeeding? Are there lactation consultants available through the hospital?

For the Baby

27. What newborn screenings are performed, and why?
28. How can I best prepare for breastfeeding and caring for my newborn?
29. What vaccinations will my baby need?

Couple Exercise #3: Prepare a List of Questions for the Doctor

Preparing a list of questions for the doctor as a couple is a beneficial exercise that can enhance communication, ensure you both are informed, and help you actively participate in prenatal visits. Here's a step-by-step guide on how to effectively create this list together:

Step 1: Set Aside Time for Discussion

Create a Comfortable Environment:

- Choose a quiet, relaxed setting where you can discuss without distractions. Make sure both of you feel comfortable and ready to engage in the conversation.

Schedule Regular Meetings:

- Set up regular times to sit down together before each prenatal visit. This helps ensure that you're both prepared and that all concerns are addressed timely.

Step 2: Gather Initial Thoughts Individually

Brainstorm Independently:

- Start by having each partner independently jot down their questions and concerns. This approach allows both of you to think freely without influence and ensures that individual concerns are respected.

Include Various Topics:

- Consider different aspects of the pregnancy such as health and symptoms, changes in lifestyle, the development of the baby, upcoming tests, and plans for labor and delivery.

Step 3: Discuss and Combine Your Lists

Share and Discuss Each List:

- Come together and discuss each item on your lists. Explain why each question is important to you, and listen attentively when your partner shares their thoughts.

Combine Lists:

- Merge your questions into a single list. Prioritize them based on importance or relevance to your stage of pregnancy.

Step 4: Research and Refine

Do Preliminary Research:

- Before finalizing your list, do some basic research to see if any of your questions can be easily answered through reliable sources like pregnancy books or reputable websites. This can help refine your questions to ensure they are specific and valuable.

Refine Your Questions:

- Make sure your questions are clear and to the point. This helps your healthcare provider understand exactly what information you are seeking.

Step 5: Organize Questions Logically

Categorize Your Questions:

- Organize your questions into categories such as health concerns, baby development, labor and delivery, and postpartum care. This can help keep the doctor's visit organized and efficient.

Prepare to Take Notes:

- Decide who will take notes during the visit or if you'll record the session (with your doctor's permission). Keeping a record helps you remember the answers and discuss them later if needed.

Step 6: Be Flexible During the Appointment

Ask the Most Important Questions First:

- Sometimes time with your doctor can be limited, so start with the most critical questions to ensure they get answered.

Be Open to Follow-up:

- If there isn't time to cover everything, ask your healthcare provider how you can follow up. Whether it's an email, a phone call, or another appointment, make sure you know how to get your remaining questions answered.

Step 7: Review Post-Visit

Discuss the Answers:

- After your visit, go over the answers together. Discuss any new information and how it affects both your feelings and plans moving forward.

Adjust Your Questions for Next Time:

- Based on what you learned, adjust any future questions or add new ones for follow-up visits.

By preparing as a couple for your prenatal visits, you not only enhance your own understanding and involvement in the pregnancy but also support each other as partners in this journey.

6. Preparing for the Baby's Arrival
Essential Shopping List for the Newborn

Preparing for the arrival of a newborn is exciting, and having a well-thought-out shopping list can make the transition smoother and less stressful. Here is an essential shopping list for your newborn to ensure you have everything you need for the early days and weeks:

Nursery Essentials

- **Crib and Mattress:** Choose a safe, comfortable crib that meets current safety standards. Invest in a firm mattress that fits snugly within the crib.
- **Bedding:** Purchase at least 2-3 fitted crib sheets and lightweight blankets. Ensure all bedding is appropriate for a baby to prevent the risk of SIDS (Sudden Infant Death Syndrome).
- **Changing Table:** A sturdy changing table with a waterproof pad and safety straps is recommended. Keep it stocked with diapers, wipes, and baby lotion or powder.
- **Baby Monitor:** A good quality baby monitor can help you keep an eye on your baby when you are not in the room.

Feeding

- **Bottles and Nipples:** Even if you plan to breastfeed, having some bottles on hand can be useful. Get different flow nipples to see what your baby prefers.
- **Breast Pump:** If you plan to breastfeed, a breast pump can help in expressing milk to feed with a bottle or to store for later use.
- **Formula:** If you plan to formula feed, stock up on a supply of formula recommended by your pediatrician.
- **Bibs and Burp Cloths:** You'll need plenty of these for feeding times to keep messes to a minimum.

Clothing

- **Onesies:** Buy several onesies in various sizes. They're comfortable for the baby and convenient for diaper changes.
- **Sleepers/Pajamas:** Get soft, comfortable pajamas that are easy to put on and take off.
- **Socks and Booties:** Keep those little feet warm with several pairs of socks or booties.
- **Hats and Mittens:** Newborns can lose a lot of heat through their heads, so hats are essential. Mittens can prevent babies from scratching themselves.

Diapering

- **Diapers:** Stock up on newborn size diapers, keeping in mind that some babies grow out of them fast. Consider starting with a box or two to adjust sizes as needed.
- **Wipes:** Unscented baby wipes are less likely to irritate the skin and are handy for diaper changes and general cleanup.
- **Diaper Rash Cream:** Have a tube of diaper rash cream ready just in case, to soothe and protect baby's skin.

Bathing

- **Baby Bathtub:** A small, baby-sized bathtub can make bath time safer and easier.
- **Baby Soap and Shampoo:** Look for gentle, baby-specific products that are hypoallergenic and free from harsh chemicals.
- **Soft Towels/Washcloths:** Soft, absorbent towels and washcloths are easier on your baby's delicate skin.

Health and Safety

- **First-Aid Kit:** Include items such as a baby thermometer, nail clippers, and a nasal aspirator.
- **Baby-Safe Laundry Detergent:** Use a detergent that is free from fragrances and dyes to wash baby's clothes and bedding.
- **Nightlight:** A soft nightlight can help during late-night feedings and diaper changes.

Travel

- **Car Seat:** A rear-facing car seat is a must for safely transporting your newborn.
- **Stroller:** Choose a stroller that's easy to handle and folds down for convenience.
- **Diaper Bag:** A good diaper bag is spacious enough to hold diapers, wipes, bottles, and extra clothes.

Preparing for a newborn can seem overwhelming, but with the right items ready and waiting, you'll be set up to focus more on enjoying your new baby. Remember, while it's tempting to buy everything at once, start with essentials and add items as you learn more about your baby's needs and preferences.

Preparing the Baby's Nursery

Preparing your baby's nursery is an exciting part of getting ready for their arrival. It involves not just decorating, but ensuring that the space is safe, comfortable, and practical. Here's a comprehensive guide to help you set up the perfect nursery:

Choosing the Room

- **Location:** Select a room that's quiet and has minimal traffic noise, away from the busiest parts of your home. It should also be conveniently located for easy access during the night.

- **Temperature:** The room should be easy to keep warm in winter and cool in summer. An even temperature helps the baby to sleep comfortably.

Safety First

- **Crib Safety:** Choose a crib that meets modern safety standards—this includes slats that are no more than 2 3/8 inches apart and no drop sides. The crib mattress should fit snugly with no gaps.

- **Secure Furniture:** Anchor all furniture to the wall, including dressers and changing tables, to prevent tipping.

- **Cord Management:** Keep cords from blinds and electrical appliances out of reach to prevent strangulation hazards.

- **Safe Toys and Decorations:** Ensure that toys are age-appropriate and that decorations are securely fastened and non-toxic.

Essential Furniture

- **Crib or Bassinet:** A sturdy crib or bassinet is the centerpiece of any nursery. Ensure it comes with a firm, flat mattress.
- **Changing Table:** A changing table with raised sides offers a safe place to change diapers. Opt for one with storage space below so you can reach diapers and wipes easily.
- **Nursing Chair:** A comfortable chair is a must-have for feeding or soothing your baby. Consider one with armrests and enough back support.

Storage Solutions

- **Clothing Storage:** A dresser or chest of drawers is essential for storing baby clothes, blankets, and other essentials. Drawer organizers can help keep smaller items tidy.
- **Shelving:** Use shelves to keep books, toys, and other necessary items within easy reach but out of the baby's hands.
- **Toy Storage:** Baskets or bins can be useful for organizing and storing toys as your baby grows.

Lighting

- **Main Lighting:** Soft, overhead lighting is sufficient for general nursery lighting.
- **Task Lighting:** Install task lighting, such as a lamp near the nursing chair for late-night feedings or changes without having to turn on the main lights.
- **Night Light:** A gentle night light can provide enough visibility for nighttime checks without disturbing the baby's sleep.

Decor

- **Color Scheme:** Choose calming, neutral colors for walls and major elements. Soft blues, greens, and pastels promote a soothing atmosphere.
- **Themed Decorations:** While themes are optional, they can be fun to design around. Popular themes include nature, nautical, floral, or geometric patterns.
- **Wall Art:** Safe, securely-mounted wall art can stimulate your baby's visual senses. Opt for pieces that are secure and can't be pulled down.

Textiles

- **Curtains:** Blackout curtains can help keep the room dark during naps and early bedtime.
- **Rugs:** A soft rug not only adds warmth to the room but also cushions the floor for when your baby starts to crawl.

- **Bedding:** Use fitted sheets in the crib and avoid loose bedding, pillows, or stuffed animals to reduce the risk of SIDS.

Ventilation and Air Quality

- **Good Air Flow:** Ensure the room is well-ventilated with clean, fresh air. Use an air purifier if necessary to maintain good air quality.
- **Humidifier:** In dry climates or during winter, a humidifier can add necessary moisture to the air and help your baby breathe easier.

Birth Planning and Choosing the Hospital

Planning for the birth of your child and choosing the right hospital are critical steps in ensuring a safe and satisfying birthing experience. Here's a comprehensive guide on how to approach these important decisions:

Birth Planning

1. Educate Yourself About the Birthing Process:

- Understanding the stages of labor and delivery can help you make informed decisions. Consider attending childbirth classes which often cover topics like labor, delivery, and postpartum care.

2. Decide on Your Birth Preferences:

- Consider different aspects such as who you want present during the birth, your pain management preferences, and positions you might prefer for labor and delivery. Document these preferences in a birth plan to discuss with your healthcare provider.

3. Discuss Your Birth Plan:

- Share your birth plan with your obstetrician or midwife during prenatal visits. They can provide feedback and help you set realistic expectations based on your health and medical history.

4. Plan for Different Scenarios:

- While having a plan is ideal, it's also important to stay flexible. Discuss potential scenarios such as induction and cesarean delivery. Understanding when these would be considered and why can prepare you for changes to the plan due to medical necessities.

Choosing the Hospital

1. Research Available Options:

- Look into hospitals or birthing centers in your area. Consider their reputations, the policies they have in place, and the types of birth they support (e.g., water birth, VBAC).

2. Consider the Proximity to Your Home:

- Choose a location that is conveniently located. Consider travel time, especially in traffic, since this could be a critical factor during labor.

3. Check Hospital Amenities and Policies:

- Investigate what each hospital offers, such as private rooms, birthing facilities, and the availability of interventions like birthing stools or epidural anesthesia.
- Learn about their policies regarding who can be in the room with you during delivery and visitation policies after the baby is born.

4. Understand Medical Staff Availability:

- Find out if you will be seen by your own doctor or a hospital staff doctor when you go into labor. Knowing who will likely deliver your baby can affect your decision.
- Ask about the availability of specialists, such as anesthesiologists and pediatricians, in case they are needed.

5. Take a Tour:

- Most hospitals offer tours of their maternity wards. Take advantage of this to see the labor and delivery rooms, postpartum rooms, and the neonatal intensive care unit (NICU) if applicable.

6. Review Maternity Care Services:

- Some hospitals provide additional services such as breastfeeding support, a maternity liaison, or postpartum support groups. Consider these services in your decision as they can be beneficial after the birth.

7. Check Insurance Coverage:

- Make sure the hospital or birthing center is covered by your health insurance. Verify what maternity and newborn care services are included in your policy to avoid unexpected costs.

8. Read Reviews and Get Recommendations:

- Look for reviews and testimonials about others' experiences at the facilities you are considering. Personal recommendations from friends or family can also provide insights into the level of care and service provided.

Making these decisions well in advance of your due date can lessen anxiety and help ensure you're in a supportive environment that aligns with your birth plan. Remember, the goal is to create a birth experience that is healthy and happy for both you and your baby.

Discussing Birth Plans and Partner's Preferences

Discussing birth plans and partner preferences is an essential step as you prepare for childbirth. It ensures that both partners feel heard, respected, and involved in the decision-making process. Here's a guide on how to approach these discussions effectively:

Understanding Birth Plans

1. What is a Birth Plan?

- A birth plan is a document that outlines your preferences for labor, delivery, and postpartum care. It typically includes details about pain management, labor positions, interventions, and who you'd like present during the delivery.

2. Why It's Important:

- A birth plan helps communicate your wishes to the healthcare team. It also prompts discussions about various childbirth scenarios, helping you to make informed choices.

Preparing for the Discussion

1. Do Your Research:

- Both partners should educate themselves about the stages of labor, common medical interventions, and potential scenarios that might arise during childbirth. This knowledge will help make the conversation more productive.

2. Gather Information:

- Review materials from childbirth classes, consult your healthcare provider, and read up on birth plan templates to understand what options might be available.

Conducting the Discussion

1. Set Aside Uninterrupted Time:

- Choose a quiet time when both partners are relaxed and can focus on the discussion without distractions.

2. Share Each Partner's Vision:

- Discuss what each of you envisions for the birth experience. This might include the environment, the use of pain relief, and preferences regarding medical interventions.

3. Discuss Key Elements of the Birth Plan:

- **Pain Management:** Talk about preferences for natural pain relief options like breathing techniques, hydrotherapy, and massage, as well as medical options such as epidurals or narcotics.

- **Labor Positions:** Explore which labor positions each partner is comfortable with and whether mobility during labor is important.

- **Medical Interventions:** Discuss under what circumstances interventions like inductions, forceps delivery, or cesareans might be acceptable.

- **After Delivery:** Talk about preferences for skin-to-skin contact, cutting the umbilical cord, and whether you plan to breastfeed immediately after birth.

- **Visitors:** Decide who you want in the delivery room and during recovery.

4. Listen Actively:

- Be open to each other's feelings and concerns. Validate each other's emotions and acknowledge that both perspectives are important.

Considerations for High-Risk Pregnancies

1. Special Scenarios:

- If your pregnancy is considered high-risk, discuss how this might affect your birth plan. Consider different scenarios that could lead to changes in the plan.

2. Flexibility:

- Understand that some aspects of the plan may need to be flexible to accommodate the health and safety of the mother and baby.

Documenting the Birth Plan

1. Write It Down:

- After the discussion, draft a birth plan that reflects the decisions you've made together. Keep it concise and clear.

2. Review with Healthcare Provider:

- Bring the birth plan to your prenatal visit and go over it with your healthcare provider. They can offer feedback and suggest any necessary revisions based on medical advisability.

Regular Reviews and Adjustments

1. Stay Flexible:

- Revisit the birth plan as the due date approaches or as circumstances change. Adjustments may be necessary as you get closer to delivery or if unexpected health issues arise.

2. Communication:

- Keep the lines of communication open. As you progress through the pregnancy, continue discussing any new feelings or concerns that arise.

Creating and discussing a birth plan together can help ensure that both partners feel prepared and supported. It builds a foundation for teamwork and shared decision-making, which is crucial as you step into parenthood together.

Couple Exercise #4: Create a Shopping List Together

Creating a shopping list together for your newborn is an engaging and practical activity that helps both partners feel involved in the preparations for the arrival of the baby. Here's how to approach this exercise to make sure it's both productive and enjoyable:

Step 1: Set a Date and Prepare

Schedule a Time:

- Choose a quiet, relaxed time when both of you can sit down together without distractions. This ensures that both partners can focus and contribute equally.

Gather Resources:

- Before you start, collect some helpful resources such as baby gear guides, recommendations from friends and family, or advice from parenting books and websites. These can provide insights into what items are essential and what can wait.

Step 2: Discuss and Prioritize Needs

Needs vs. Wants:

- Start by differentiating between what you need immediately after the baby's arrival and what might be nice to have. Essentials might include items like a car seat, crib, diapers, and basic clothing. Wants could be things like a high-end stroller or designer baby clothes.

Review and Research Products:

- Discuss each item's necessity, safety, and space requirements. Consider doing some quick online research together to read reviews or compare prices and features.

Step 3: Create Categories

Organize by Category:

- Divide your list into categories such as Nursery, Feeding, Diapering, Clothing, Travel, and Health. This helps in making the shopping process more organized and ensures no essential category is overlooked.

Step 4: Compile the List

Write It Down:

- As you discuss each category, write down the items you agree to purchase. Use a shared document or app where both can view and edit the list, such as a Google Doc or a shared notetaking app.

Assign Tasks:

- Decide who will research and buy each item, or if you'll do it together. Assigning tasks can help divide the workload and make the process more manageable.

Step 5: Set a Budget

Discuss Finances:

- It's important to set a realistic budget for your baby supplies. Discuss how much you are willing to spend overall and on big-ticket items.

Look for Deals:

- Plan to shop during sales, use coupons, or check out second-hand stores for some items to stay within your budget.

Step 6: Plan Shopping Dates

Decide When and Where to Shop:

- Determine whether you will shop online or in-store. Set specific dates for shopping trips or online research sessions.

Step 7: Review and Adjust

Flexibility:

- Be prepared to adjust your list as you go. You might find some items unnecessary or discover new needs as you get closer to your due date.

Check Off Items:

- As you purchase items, check them off your list. This will give you a clear idea of what's left and prevent duplicate purchases.

Step 8: Celebrate and Reflect

Enjoy the Process:

- Make the shopping and preparation part of your celebration as expecting parents. Enjoy each step, from researching to setting up the nursery.

Reflect on the Experience:

- After completing the list, reflect on how the process worked for you as a couple. Discuss what you enjoyed and how you could improve other joint projects in the future.

By creating a shopping list together, you can ensure that both partners are actively involved in the preparations, making decisions together, and sharing the excitement and responsibility of welcoming a new member to your family.

7. Labor and Postpartum

Signs of Labor and When to Go to the Hospital

Recognizing the signs of labor and knowing when to head to the hospital are crucial as you approach your due date. Here's a detailed guide to help you identify true labor signs and decide when it's time to go to the hospital.

Signs of Labor

1. Contractions:

- **Regular and Increasing Intensity:** Unlike Braxton Hicks contractions, which are irregular and typically painless, true labor contractions come at regular intervals and gradually get closer together and stronger.
- **Consistency in Frequency:** Contractions that come every 5-10 minutes and last about 60 seconds are a strong indicator of labor. They don't ease with movement or changing positions.

2. Water Breaking:

- **Leak or Gush of Fluid:** Your membranes may rupture, resulting in a continuous leak or a sudden gush of clear or slightly pink fluid. This can happen before contractions start or during labor.
- **What to Do:** If you think your water has broken, call your healthcare provider immediately. Most women go into labor within 24 hours after their water breaks. If contractions don't start on their own, labor might be induced to avoid infection.

3. Effacement and Dilation:

- **Thinning and Opening of the Cervix:** As labor approaches, the cervix begins to thin (efface) and open (dilate). Your healthcare provider can assess this through a vaginal exam.

4. Bloody Show:

- **Mucus Plug and Blood:** The discharge of the mucus plug that blocks the cervix during pregnancy may occur. It can be clear, pink, or slightly bloody and is a sign that labor could start soon.

5. Nesting Instinct:

- **Sudden Burst of Energy:** Some women experience a burst of energy and an urge to "nest" or prepare the home for the baby's arrival.

When to Go to the Hospital

1. Contractions:

- **Rule of Thumb:** A common guideline is to head to the hospital when contractions are 5 minutes apart, lasting 60 seconds, and consistent for at least 1 hour, especially for first-time mothers.
- **High-Risk Pregnancy:** If you have a high-risk pregnancy, your doctor might give you specific instructions that differ from typical advice.

2. Water Breaks:

- **No Contractions:** If your water breaks but you don't have contractions, contact your healthcare provider. They will likely advise you to come to the hospital to avoid the risk of infection.

3. Vaginal Bleeding:

- **More than a Bloody Show:** If you experience significant bleeding, it's essential to go to the hospital immediately as this could indicate a complication.

4. Decreased Fetal Movement:

- **Less Activity from the Baby:** If you notice that the baby is moving less than usual, it's important to contact your healthcare provider or go to the hospital to ensure the baby is not in distress.

5. Any Concerns or Uncertainty:

- **When in Doubt:** If you're unsure whether you are in labor or if you feel something isn't right, it's always safe to call your healthcare provider for advice.

Being prepared and knowing what to look for as labor approaches can help alleviate some of the anxiety associated with the onset of labor. Always have a plan in place for getting to the hospital and keep your healthcare provider's contact information handy as your due date approaches.

Father's Role During Labor and Delivery

The role of a father during labor and delivery is crucial and can significantly impact the overall birthing experience for both the mother and the baby. Fathers can provide emotional support, physical comfort, and practical assistance. Here's a guide to help fathers prepare for an active and supportive role during labor and delivery:

Before Labor Begins

1. Educate Yourself:

- Understand the stages of labor and common medical procedures or interventions that might occur. Knowledge about what to expect can reduce anxiety and enable you to be a more effective supporter.

2. Prepare for the Hospital:

- Help pack the hospital bag, ensuring it includes items for both the mother and yourself, such as clothing, toiletries, snacks, and any comforts of home like pillows or photos.

3. Plan the Logistics:

- Know the route to the hospital and have a backup plan. Ensure the car has enough fuel, and you understand where to park and where to go once you arrive at the hospital.

During Labor

1. Provide Emotional Support:

- Offer constant reassurance and encouragement. Labor can be intense, and emotional support is incredibly valuable. Be present, hold her hand, and help maintain a calm and supportive environment.

2. Advocate for Her Wishes:

- Help communicate her birth plan and preferences to the medical staff. Ensure her wishes are respected as much as possible, stepping in to speak on her behalf if she is unable to do so.

3. Assist with Comfort Measures:

- Help her change positions to find the most comfortable position for labor. Use massage, pressure, or counterpressure to relieve pain. Assist with breathing techniques if you've practiced them together.

4. Stay Informed:

- Keep track of what's happening during labor and delivery. Ask questions if things aren't clear so you can relay accurate information to the mother, helping her make informed decisions.

During Delivery

1. Be an Active Participant:

- If both of you are comfortable and it's allowed, be present at the moment of delivery. You might be able to support her physically as she pushes or provide verbal encouragement.

2. Cut the Umbilical Cord:

- If you are interested and it's part of the birth plan, you might have the opportunity to cut the umbilical cord.

3. Capture the Moment:

- If desired, take photos or videos of the first moments post-birth. However, always prioritize being mentally and emotionally present over documenting the experience.

After Delivery

1. Skin-to-Skin Contact:

- If the mother is unable, you might be able to hold the newborn against your skin. This can help calm and soothe the baby and is a great way to begin bonding.

2. Support with Feeding:

- Assist with breastfeeding or bottle-feeding. Help position the baby and bring the mother anything she needs during feeding.

3. Communicate with Family and Friends:

- Handle communications with eager family and friends. Share the news and any updates when appropriate.

Ongoing Support

1. Keep Providing Support:

- The first few hours and days after delivery are a time of significant adjustment. Continue to provide emotional and practical support, helping with diaper changes, soothing the baby, and ensuring the mother has time to rest and recover.

Being an involved and supportive father during labor and delivery can enhance the childbirth experience and strengthen the bond among you, your partner, and your newborn. Remember, your role is vital, and your presence is a source of strength and comfort.

Caring for Your Partner After Birth

Caring for your partner after the birth of your baby is crucial, as it can significantly impact her recovery and the overall adjustment to parenthood. Here are practical ways to provide support and ensure the postpartum period is as smooth and comfortable as possible for both of you:

Physical Care

1. Help with Recovery:

- **Understand the Recovery Process:** Familiarize yourself with the typical recovery timeline and signs of complications, such as excessive bleeding, infection, or prolonged emotional distress.
- **Assist with Daily Needs:** Take on more responsibilities around the house, such as cooking, cleaning, and shopping, so your partner can focus on recovery and bonding with the baby.

2. Manage Pain and Discomfort:

- **Administer Medications:** Keep track of any prescribed pain medications or over-the-counter drugs recommended by her healthcare provider.
- **Provide Comfort Measures:** Help with ice packs, heating pads, or comfortable seating arrangements to ease pain and swelling.

Emotional Support

1. Encourage Rest and Sleep:

- **Take Shifts with the Baby:** Share responsibilities for baby care during the night so your partner can get uninterrupted sleep.
- **Create a Restful Environment:** Ensure the sleeping area is quiet, dark, and comfortable to facilitate better sleep.

2. Listen and Communicate:

- **Provide Emotional Support:** Be a good listener, allowing her to express feelings and frustrations without offering solutions unless asked.
- **Encourage Open Communication:** Discuss both your feelings about parenthood, changes in your relationship, and household responsibilities to ensure both of you feel supported and understood.

Nutritional Support

1. Healthy Meals:

- **Prepare Nutritious Foods:** Cook and provide meals rich in nutrients necessary for postpartum recovery, such as protein, vitamins, and iron, which are crucial, especially if she is breastfeeding.
- **Stay Hydrated:** Keep her supplied with plenty of fluids, especially water, to help with recovery and lactation.

Bonding with the Baby

1. Encourage Bonding:

- **Support Her in Baby Care:** Help her feel confident in her mothering skills by being positive and encouraging about her interactions with the baby.
- **Facilitate Mother-Baby Bonding:** Give her and the baby space to bond, particularly during feeding times, whether she's breastfeeding or bottle-feeding.

Support with Breastfeeding

1. Breastfeeding Assistance:

- **Learn About Breastfeeding:** Educate yourself about common breastfeeding issues and how to address them, so you can offer practical help or suggest seeking help from a lactation consultant if challenges arise.
- **Provide Physical Comfort:** Bring her pillows, a drink, or a snack while she breastfeeds, and make sure she is comfortable.

Handling Visits

1. Manage Expectations with Visitors:

- **Coordinate Visits:** Help manage family and friends' expectations regarding visits to ensure she has enough rest and privacy.
- **Act as a Buffer:** Politely enforce visiting rules that you both have agreed upon to maintain a peaceful environment.

Professional Help

1. Encourage Professional Consultation:

- **Be Observant of Her Health:** Watch for signs of postpartum depression or any physical health issues that seem unusual or persistent.
- **Encourage Seeking Help:** If she exhibits signs of emotional or physical health issues, encourage her to see a healthcare provider.

Overall, being attentive, proactive, and involved in household and baby care tasks can significantly ease your partner's postpartum recovery. Most importantly, ensure that she feels loved and supported during this transitional and often challenging time.

Involvement in the First Weeks of the Baby's Life

Being actively involved in the first few weeks of your baby's life is crucial not just for the baby's development and bonding, but also for supporting your partner and sharing the responsibilities of new parenthood. Here's how you can be effectively involved during this critical period:

Direct Care for the Baby

1. Feeding:

- Whether your partner is breastfeeding or bottle-feeding, you can assist by bringing the baby to her, handling the bottle feedings, or taking over burping the baby afterward.
- If she's breastfeeding, bring her water, snacks, or anything else she might need, and make sure she is comfortable.

2. Diaper Changing:

- Share the responsibility for diaper changes. Becoming proficient in diapering not only gives you valuable bonding time with your baby but also provides significant relief for your partner.

3. Soothing and Bonding:

- Learn how to soothe the baby through rocking, singing, or gentle patting. Skin-to-skin contact isn't just for mothers; it's also beneficial when fathers practice it, helping to build a strong emotional connection with their newborn.

4. Establishing Sleep Routines:

- Take turns getting up with the baby during the night so both of you can get some rest. Learn how to soothe the baby back to sleep, which is invaluable for your partner's recovery.

Supporting Your Partner

1. Encouragement and Empathy:

- Understand the physical and emotional changes your partner is going through and provide emotional support. Listening to her concerns without judgment can be one of the most crucial supports you provide.

2. Help Around the House:

- Take on more household duties like cooking, cleaning, and laundry. Keeping the home environment stress-free can significantly help both of you focus more on the baby and less on chores.

3. Coordinate Visits:

- Help manage the flow of visitors to ensure that they don't overwhelm your partner or disrupt the baby's routine. It's important to prioritize your family's needs during this time.

Personal Involvement

1. Education:

- Continue educating yourself about newborn care. Understanding the stages of newborn development and common issues can make you more confident and proactive.

2. Record Keeping:

- Take charge of recording important information such as feeding times, sleep patterns, and diaper changes. This can help in pediatric visits and understand your baby's habits and needs.

3. Capture Moments:

- Take photos and videos to document these early weeks. These are cherished memories, and taking the initiative means your partner can focus more on recovery and care.

Professional Guidance

1. Pediatric Appointments:

- Be present for pediatric appointments. This shows your involvement and ensures you're equally informed about health issues, vaccinations, and growth milestones.

2. Mental Health:

- Be aware of the signs of postpartum depression both in your partner and yourself. If you notice potential symptoms, encourage seeking help from a healthcare provider.

Being involved in the early weeks of your baby's life sets a foundation for continued engagement throughout your child's development and strengthens the co-parenting bond between you and your partner. It is a critical time to establish routines, share responsibilities, and support each other as you navigate the new realities of parenting together.

Couple Exercise #5: Discuss and Plan for the Birth Day

Discussing and planning for the birth day together is a vital step in ensuring that both partners feel prepared, supported, and involved. This exercise can help reduce anxiety about the delivery and foster a deeper connection between partners as they transition into parenthood. Here's how to effectively plan this discussion:

Step 1: Set Aside Dedicated Time

Choose a calm, comfortable setting where you won't be interrupted. Ensure that both partners feel relaxed and ready to focus on the discussion without distractions.

Step 2: Gather Information

Before the discussion, gather all necessary information about the birthing process, options available at your birthing center or hospital, and any policies that might affect your birth plan. This might include visitor policies, available pain relief options, and what typically happens during labor and delivery at your chosen facility.

Step 3: Discuss Each Other's Hopes and Concerns

Start the conversation by sharing your hopes and fears about the birth day.

- **For the birthing partner:** Discuss your desires for pain management, who you want present during the delivery, and how you envision the labor and delivery process.
- **For the supporting partner:** Share how you hope to be involved, any anxieties about the delivery, and how you think you can best support your partner during labor.

Step 4: Create a Birth Plan Together

Using the information and preferences discussed, start drafting a birth plan. Include decisions on key issues such as:

- **Pain management:** Options like natural pain relief, epidurals, or other medications.
- **Labor preferences:** Include preferences for walking, using a birthing ball, and positions for delivery.
- **Role of the partner:** Specify how the non-birthing partner wishes to be involved—whether that's holding a hand, providing words of encouragement, or cutting the umbilical cord.
- **Atmosphere in the room:** Discuss the environment you both want, like playing specific music, dimming the lights, or having particular items from home.

- **Medical interventions:** Talk about scenarios where interventions such as inductions or cesarean sections might be necessary and under what conditions you both would feel comfortable with these options.

Step 5: Review and Modify the Plan

Understand that the birth plan is a guide, not a contract. It's important to remain flexible as situations during labor can change quickly. Discuss how you'll handle deviations from the plan if they arise.

Step 6: Communicate the Plan with Your Healthcare Provider

Schedule an appointment to go over your birth plan with your healthcare provider. They can provide insights, suggest adjustments based on medical advisability, and confirm what's possible in your birthing environment.

Step 7: Prepare Logistically

Discuss and decide on practical matters such as:

- **When to leave for the hospital:** Know the signs of labor and decide at what point you will go to the hospital.
- **Packing a hospital bag:** Ensure you have everything you'll need, like clothes for both mother and baby, snacks, and any comfort items.
- **Transportation and communication:** Plan who will drive to the hospital, how you'll communicate your progress to family and friends, and who will handle updates during and after labor.

Step 8: Reflect and Adjust

After discussing and planning, take some time to reflect. Are there any areas where one partner feels uncomfortable or uncertain? Address these concerns and adjust the plan accordingly.

Step 9: Practice and Visualize

Spend some time practicing scenarios, like how to time contractions and when to implement different comfort measures. Visualization can also help both partners feel more prepared and relaxed about the upcoming birth.

By actively participating in this planning exercise, both partners can feel more connected and supportive as they approach the exciting moment of meeting their new baby. This collaborative approach ensures that both voices are heard and respected, setting a strong foundation for teamwork in parenting.

8. Parenthood and Relationships
Strengthening the Couple's Relationship

Strengthening your relationship during pregnancy and after the arrival of a baby is crucial, as this period can significantly strain even the strongest partnerships. Here are some effective strategies to help couples maintain and enhance their relationship during these transformative times:

Open and Honest Communication

1. Regular Check-ins:

- Establish a routine where you both share your feelings, concerns, and experiences. This can be a dedicated time each day or week where you focus solely on communicating with each other.

2. Active Listening:

- Practice active listening by giving your full attention, acknowledging your partner's feelings, and responding thoughtfully. Avoid interrupting or planning your response while your partner is speaking.

Shared Experiences and Quality Time

1. Date Nights:

- Continue to prioritize date nights, whether at home or out. These can be simple, such as a movie night or a walk together, but the focus should be on connecting without distractions.

2. Shared Hobbies and Interests:

- Engage in activities you both enjoy or start a new hobby together. This can be anything from cooking classes to sports, which can help strengthen your bond and provide a break from parenting duties.

Emotional Support and Understanding

1. Empathy and Support:

- Be empathetic towards each other's experiences and challenges during pregnancy and early parenthood. Recognize that both partners may face stress and emotional upheaval, albeit in different ways.

2. Validate Each Other's Feelings:

- Validate each other's feelings without judgment. Acknowledge that it's okay to feel overwhelmed, tired, or anxious, and offer support and understanding.

Physical Intimacy and Affection

1. Maintain Physical Closeness:

- Keep physical intimacy alive, according to comfort levels, which might change especially after childbirth. Hugs, kisses, and cuddles can significantly enhance emotional connection.

2. Discuss Changes in Intimacy:

- Openly discuss any changes in sexual desires or physical limitations due to pregnancy or postpartum recovery. Adjust your intimate life accordingly and seek professional advice if needed.

Conflict Resolution

1. Address Issues Promptly:

- Don't let resentments build up. Address misunderstandings or conflicts as they arise with the aim of resolving them constructively.

2. Use 'I' Statements:

- Communicate issues and feelings without blame. Use "I" statements to express how you feel and what you need, rather than pointing out what your partner is doing wrong.

Planning and Collaboration

1. Parenting Decisions:

- Make parenting decisions together. Discuss and agree on key parenting issues like discipline, education, and values to ensure consistency and mutual support.

2. Co-Parenting Duties:

- Share parenting duties fairly to prevent burnout and resentment. Actively participating in daily childcare tasks can promote equality and partnership.

Seeking External Support

1. Couples Counseling:

- Consider couples counseling if you find it challenging to resolve issues on your own. A professional can provide neutral guidance and help strengthen your relationship.

2. Social Support:

- Lean on friends, family, or parent groups for support. External support can provide relief and new perspectives on managing the challenges of parenthood.

By actively working to strengthen your relationship through these strategies, you can better navigate the joys and challenges of parenthood together, ensuring a healthy environment for your new family.

Effective Communication and Conflict Management

Effective communication and conflict management are essential skills for maintaining a healthy relationship, especially during times of stress such as pregnancy or the early stages of parenting. Here are strategies to improve communication and manage conflicts effectively:

Building Effective Communication

1. Practice Active Listening:

- Focus on truly listening to your partner without planning your response while they are speaking. This involves giving full attention, nodding, and using affirmations like "I understand" to show engagement.

2. Express Yourself Clearly and Honestly:

- Use "I" statements to express your thoughts and feelings. For example, say "I feel overwhelmed when..." instead of "You make me feel overwhelmed..." This helps prevent your partner from feeling attacked and keeps the focus on your experiences.

3. Validate Each Other's Feelings:

- Acknowledge your partner's emotions by validating their feelings. Even if you don't agree with their perspective, recognizing their feelings can make them feel heard and supported.

4. Keep Communication Open and Regular:

- Don't let busy schedules stop you from communicating. Set aside regular times to check in with each other, ensuring you both can talk about any issues or share how you're feeling.

Conflict Management Strategies

1. Identify the Real Issue:

- Often, conflicts escalate because the underlying issue isn't addressed. Try to identify the root cause of the disagreement instead of arguing over symptoms of the problem.

2. Take a Time-Out if Needed:

- If emotions become too heated, it's okay to take a break from the discussion. Agree to pause the conversation and come back when both partners are calmer and more composed.

3. Use Problem-Solving Techniques:

- Approach conflicts with a problem-solving mindset. Discuss possible solutions and compromises together, aiming to find an outcome that satisfies both partners.

4. Avoid Blame and Accusations:

- Stay away from blaming or accusing language, which can lead to defensiveness and shut down productive conversation. Focus on discussing behaviors and outcomes rather than personality traits.

Enhancing Conflict Resolution

1. Establish Ground Rules:

- Set clear guidelines for how to handle disagreements. This might include no yelling, no interrupting, or no going to bed angry. Ground rules can help keep conflicts constructive.

2. Focus on the Present:

- Try not to bring up past arguments. Focusing on the current issue helps prevent the discussion from becoming overwhelming and unmanageable.

3. Seek to Understand Before Being Understood:

- Make an effort to understand your partner's point of view before trying to get your point across. This can help you empathize with their position and facilitate a more effective resolution.

4. Commit to Making Changes:

- If the conflict arises from behaviors that one or both partners can change, commit to making those changes. Follow through is crucial for building trust and ensuring issues do not recur.

Seeking Help When Needed

1. Consider Couples Therapy:

- If conflicts frequently escalate or you find it difficult to resolve issues on your own, consider seeking help from a couples therapist. Professional guidance can provide new tools and perspectives.

Effective communication and conflict management are ongoing processes that require attention and effort. By continually working on these skills, you can strengthen your relationship and create a more harmonious home environment, especially important when navigating the challenges of raising a family.

Dividing Household Tasks and Baby Care

Dividing household tasks and baby care responsibilities effectively is crucial for maintaining a balanced and supportive relationship, especially with the added pressures of a new baby. Here's a guide to help couples share these duties in a fair and efficient way:

Communication and Planning

1. Open Discussion:

- Begin with an open discussion about household responsibilities. Acknowledge each partner's current commitments, such as work hours and personal obligations, to gauge how tasks can be equitably divided.

2. Create a List:

- Write down all household tasks (cleaning, cooking, shopping, etc.) and all aspects of baby care (feeding, diapering, bedtime routines). This visual representation helps ensure no task is overlooked.

3. Set Priorities:

- Identify which tasks are most critical and how often they need to be done. This will help in assigning responsibilities according to each partner's preferences and strengths.

Fair Division of Labor

1. Equitable, Not Necessarily Equal:

- Division of labor should be fair, considering each partner's workload outside the home, energy levels, and personal strengths. It may not always be a 50/50 split, but it should feel equitable to both partners.

2. Match Tasks with Preferences and Skills:

- Whenever possible, align tasks with each partner's preferences and skills. For example, if one partner enjoys cooking, they might take on more cooking duties, while the other handles different tasks.

3. Rotate Responsibilities:

- Consider rotating less desirable chores so that no one person is always stuck with the same tedious tasks. This can help keep resentment from building up.

Planning for Baby Care

1. Scheduling:

- Create a schedule for baby-related tasks, especially for things like night feedings and changing diapers. Decide who does what and when, possibly taking shifts if it helps manage sleep deprivation better.

2. Flexibility:

- Keep the schedule flexible. Needs can change rapidly with a newborn, so be prepared to adjust as you learn more about your baby's habits and needs.

3. Shared Activities:

- Ensure both parents have opportunities for bonding with the baby through shared activities like baths, bedtime stories, and playtime. This not only helps with bonding but also gives both parents confidence in handling the baby.

Using Tools and Resources

1. Shared Calendars:

- Use digital calendars or apps to keep track of who is doing what each day. This can help manage schedules and avoid confusion or overlap.

2. Apps for Chore Management:

- Consider apps designed for managing household chores which can be used to assign tasks, set reminders, and track completion.

Regular Reviews

1. Weekly Check-ins:

- Have a weekly discussion to review how the task sharing is going. Discuss what's working and what isn't, and make adjustments as needed. This is also a good time to address any feelings of imbalance or dissatisfaction.

2. Acknowledgment and Appreciation:

- Regularly acknowledge each other's contributions and express appreciation. Recognizing each other's efforts can go a long way in maintaining a positive and supportive relationship.

Professional Help

1. Consider Outside Help:

- If budget allows, consider hiring outside help for certain tasks like cleaning. This can alleviate stress and free up time for both parents to relax or spend quality time with the baby.

By effectively dividing household and baby care tasks, both partners can feel supported and less overwhelmed, leading to a healthier and happier home environment. This collaborative approach also sets a strong foundation for teamwork in family life.

Importance of Quality Family Time

Quality family time is crucial for building strong bonds, creating lasting memories, and supporting each other's emotional well-being. Here's why prioritizing this time is essential, particularly in a family setting:

Strengthening Family Bonds

Spending quality time together strengthens the emotional connections between family members. It helps build a sense of belonging and security, especially important for children as they grow and develop. Regular family interactions foster a supportive environment where members feel valued and understood.

Communication and Understanding

Quality time allows family members to communicate openly, share their thoughts and feelings, and stay connected with each other's lives. This open line of communication can help prevent misunderstandings and resolve conflicts more effectively, as everyone becomes more attuned to each other's needs and perspectives.

Educational Benefits

For children, family time can be both fun and educational. Parents and siblings can engage in activities that promote learning, such as reading, playing educational games, or exploring nature together. These activities not only teach new skills but also demonstrate the value of learning in a supportive and relaxed environment.

Stress Relief and Mental Health

In today's fast-paced world, spending time with family can be a significant stress reliever for all ages. It provides a break from the pressures of school, work, and social commitments, allowing family members to relax, laugh, and enjoy each other's company. This downtime is essential for maintaining mental health and emotional resilience.

Building Life Skills

Family time often involves activities that require teamwork, problem-solving, and communication. Whether it's planning a family outing, cooking a meal together, or solving a puzzle, these activities help children and adults alike develop essential life skills in a supportive setting.

Creating Memories

Quality family time creates cherished memories that strengthen familial ties. Celebrations, vacations, and even simple daily activities like evening walks or bedtime stories become part of a family's shared history, enhancing the sense of identity and continuity.

Modeling Behavior

For children, observing how their parents and older siblings handle various situations during family interactions serves as an important behavioral model. Through family time, parents can set examples of empathy, patience, and respect, which children are likely to emulate.

Maintaining Rituals and Traditions

Family traditions, whether they're related to holidays, birthdays, or weekly routines like Sunday dinners, play a crucial role in shaping a family's cultural identity and provide a sense of rhythm and predictability that can be comforting in a chaotic world.

Adjusting and Adapting

Quality family time provides opportunities to check in with each other and adjust to any changes within the family dynamic, such as moves, changes in jobs, or developmental stages. Regular interaction helps families adapt to these changes more smoothly, ensuring everyone feels supported through transitions.

Prioritizing and Planning Family Time

Given the benefits, it's important to prioritize and plan for family time:

- **Schedule It:** Make family time a regular and non-negotiable part of your calendar.
- **Be Present:** During family activities, focus on being fully present, setting aside electronic devices and distractions.
- **Include Everyone:** Make sure activities are inclusive, considering all family members' interests and abilities.
- **Keep It Simple:** Family time doesn't need to be elaborate or expensive. Even everyday activities can be meaningful.

By making quality family time a priority, families can enjoy all these benefits, leading to a happier, healthier family life.

Couple Exercise #6: Schedule Quality Time Together

Scheduling quality time together as a couple is essential, especially during busy periods like preparing for a new baby or managing the dynamics of family life. Here's a step-by-step guide on how to effectively plan and ensure you have meaningful moments together:

Step 1: Acknowledge the Importance

Start by acknowledging the importance of spending quality time together for both your relationship and individual well-being. Recognize that maintaining a strong bond is crucial and requires effort and planning.

Step 2: Discuss Preferences and Interests

Share Interests:

- Discuss what activities you both enjoy. Whether it's a hobby you used to share or something new you'd like to try together, finding common interests is key.

Explore New Ideas:

- Consider trying something new that neither of you has done but both are curious about. This could be a class, a sport, or a creative activity.

Step 3: Create a Schedule

Set a Regular Date and Time:

- Choose a regular day and time for your quality time, treating it as important as any other appointment or commitment. Whether it's weekly or bi-weekly, consistency is important.

Plan Around Obstacles:

- Anticipate potential obstacles such as work schedules, family commitments, or other responsibilities, and plan your quality time accordingly.

Step 4: Plan Activities

Mix Routine and Special Activities:

- Alternate between simple activities like walking in the park, cooking a meal together, or watching a movie, and more planned events like dining out, attending a concert, or a day trip.

Keep a List:

- Keep a running list of activities that you both would like to do. This can make planning easier and ensures you have a variety of options to keep things interesting.

Step 5: Be Flexible but Committed

Stay Flexible:

- While it's important to stick to your schedule, be flexible about what you do during your quality time. Sometimes just being together is enough.

Stay Committed:

- Treat these moments as sacred. Avoid canceling or rescheduling unless absolutely necessary to show that your relationship is a priority.

Step 6: Limit Distractions

Unplug:

- Agree to unplug from phones, computers, and other electronic devices. This helps both of you to be fully present and engaged during your time together.

Step 7: Evaluate and Adjust

Regular Check-ins:

- Have regular check-ins to discuss how your scheduled quality time is going. Talk about what you've enjoyed and what might need changing.

Keep Improving:

- Be open to adjusting the frequency, timing, or types of activities based on how your lives and interests evolve.

Step 8: Show Appreciation

Express Gratitude:

- Regularly express appreciation for each other and the effort involved in maintaining your relationship through these scheduled times.

Celebrate Milestones:

- Use these quality times to celebrate milestones in your relationship or personal life. Recognizing and celebrating these can enhance your connection.

By carefully planning and committing to regular quality time, couples can maintain a strong, healthy relationship amid the complexities of everyday life. This structured approach ensures that both partners feel valued and connected, which is especially important in times of change or stress.

9. Practical Aspects of Fatherhood
Diaper Changing and Feeding the Newborn

Changing diapers and feeding are two of the most fundamental tasks you'll undertake with your newborn. Both are not only essential care activities but also important bonding experiences. Here's a detailed guide on how to manage these responsibilities effectively:

Diaper Changing

1. Setup Your Changing Station:

- Have a dedicated changing area that is safe, clean, and well-stocked with all necessary supplies: diapers, wipes, diaper rash cream, and a changing pad with safety straps.
- Keep everything within reach to ensure you don't have to leave your baby unattended at any time.

2. Safe Changing Practices:

- Always keep one hand on your baby while they are on the changing table.
- Never leave your baby unattended on a high surface, even for a moment.
- Dispose of diapers properly to maintain hygiene and prevent odors.

3. Diaper Changing Steps:

- Lay your baby down on their back on the changing pad.
- Remove the dirty diaper and use the front half to wipe away the bulk of the mess.
- Use baby wipes to clean the area thoroughly but gently; always wipe from front to back to prevent infection, especially in girls.
- Apply diaper rash cream if there are any signs of redness or rash.
- Lift your baby's legs by the ankles and slide a clean diaper underneath. The back of the diaper should be level with your baby's belly button.
- Fasten the diaper snugly but ensure it isn't too tight to cause discomfort or marks on their skin.

4. Regular Checks:

- Newborns need frequent diaper changes to prevent diaper rash and discomfort. Check the diaper every two hours or so, and always after feedings.

Feeding the Newborn

1. Breastfeeding Basics:

- Find a comfortable position for both you and your baby. Common positions include the cradle hold, football hold, and side-lying position.
- Ensure your baby latches on properly to prevent nipple soreness and allow effective feeding. The baby's mouth should cover both the nipple and much of the areola.
- Breastfeed on demand (usually every 2-3 hours) to establish a good milk supply.

2. Formula Feeding Guidelines:

- Choose an iron-fortified formula unless advised otherwise by your pediatrician.
- Prepare bottles according to the manufacturer's instructions, ensuring they are sterile.
- Hold your baby semi-upright and tilt the bottle so the milk fills the neck of the bottle and covers the nipple. This prevents your baby from swallowing air.
- Like breastfeeding, feed your baby every 2-3 hours or as needed.

3. Signs Your Baby is Hungry:

- Early signs of hunger include stirring, stretching, sucking motions, and lip movements.
- Crying is a late indicator of hunger. Try to feed before your baby becomes distressed.

4. Burping Your Baby:

- Whether breastfeeding or bottle-feeding, burp your baby during and after each feeding. This can be done by holding your baby upright against your chest with their chin over your shoulder and patting their back gently.
- You can also sit your baby on your lap, supporting their chest and head with one hand while patting their back with the other.

5. Monitoring Feeding:

- Keep track of your baby's feeding times and duration. Also, note their diaper output: expect about six wet diapers a day and at least three bowel movements once milk supply is established.

Both diaper changing and feeding provide excellent opportunities for skin-to-skin contact and to strengthen the emotional bond between you and your baby. Handling these activities with care and patience lays a foundation for a nurturing and secure relationship.

Sleep Patterns and Managing Sleepless Nights

Managing sleep patterns and dealing with sleepless nights are common challenges for new parents. Here's how you can approach these issues effectively, ensuring both your baby and you get as much rest as possible:

Understanding Newborn Sleep Patterns

1. Sleep Phases:

- Newborns sleep a lot, typically 14 to 17 hours a day, but their sleep occurs in short bursts throughout a 24-hour period. This is because their internal clocks aren't fully developed yet.
- Sleep cycles for newborns are shorter and include more REM (Rapid Eye Movement) sleep, which is necessary for the incredible development happening in their brains.

2. Development of Sleep Patterns:

- Over the first few months, your baby will gradually start to sleep for longer periods at night. By the age of 3 to 4 months, some babies can sleep at least five hours at a stretch.

Strategies for Managing Sleepless Nights

1. Share Nighttime Duties:

- If possible, take turns tending to the baby at night so each parent can get a longer stretch of uninterrupted sleep. If breastfeeding, a non-breastfeeding partner can handle diaper changes and soothing the baby back to sleep after feedings.

2. Create a Bedtime Routine:

- Establishing a consistent bedtime routine can help signal to your baby that it's time to wind down and rest. This routine might include a warm bath, a quiet feeding, cuddling, and a lullaby or gentle music.

3. Optimize Your Bedroom Environment:

- Ensure your bedroom is conducive to sleep for both you and the baby. Use blackout curtains to keep the room dark, a white noise machine to drown out household noise, and maintain a comfortable temperature.

4. Practice Safe Co-Sleeping or Room Sharing:

- The American Academy of Pediatrics recommends room-sharing for at least the first six months. This setup makes nighttime feedings easier and has been shown to reduce the risk of SIDS (Sudden Infant Death Syndrome). Make sure each sleeping arrangement follows safety guidelines to prevent accidents.

Coping with Sleep Deprivation

1. Nap When Your Baby Naps:

- Try to rest or take naps during the day when your baby sleeps, rather than using this time to catch up on household chores.

2. Seek Help:

- Don't hesitate to ask family or friends for help to allow you to get some rest. Sometimes a few hours of uninterrupted sleep can make a significant difference.

3. Keep Nights Low-Key:

- Keep the lights dim and the environment quiet during nighttime feedings and changes. This helps maintain your baby's understanding that night is for sleeping.

4. Watch for Sleep Cues:

- Put your baby to bed as soon as you notice signs of sleepiness like rubbing eyes, yawning, or looking away. Over-tired babies have a harder time falling and staying asleep.

When to Seek Professional Help

1. Persistent Sleep Issues:

- If you're concerned about your baby's sleep patterns or your ability to cope with sleep deprivation, consult with your pediatrician. They can check for underlying issues and offer guidance or refer you to a sleep specialist.

2. Signs of Postpartum Depression:

- Significant sleep deprivation can exacerbate postpartum mood disorders. If you or your partner are feeling overwhelmed, excessively tired, or hopeless, seek professional help.

Understanding and managing sleep in the early months of parenting can be challenging but knowing what to expect and how to handle sleepless nights can make a big difference. Be patient as you and your baby learn to navigate these early stages together.

Newborn Safety at Home and Outside

Ensuring the safety of a newborn both at home and when outside is paramount for any parent. Here are comprehensive tips and practices to help keep your newborn safe in various environments.

Safety at Home

1. Safe Sleeping Environment:

- Always place your baby on their back to sleep on a firm, flat surface like a crib or bassinet with a tight-fitting sheet.
- Keep pillows, blankets, stuffed toys, and bumpers out of the crib to prevent suffocation risks.

2. Babyproofing:

- Babyproof your home before your baby starts crawling. Cover electrical outlets, secure cords, install gates at staircases, and ensure furniture and TVs are anchored to prevent tipping.
- Keep small objects, which are a choking hazard, out of reach.

3. Bath Time Safety:

- Never leave your baby unattended in the bath, even for a second. Always test the water temperature with your wrist or elbow to ensure it's not too hot.
- Use a baby bathtub with a non-slip surface and keep bath supplies within reach.

4. Smoke and Carbon Monoxide Detectors:

- Install smoke and carbon monoxide detectors in your home and check them regularly to ensure they are working properly.

5. Avoid Overheating:

- Monitor the room temperature where your baby sleeps and dress them appropriately to avoid overheating. Ideal room temperature for a baby is generally considered to be between 68-72°F (20-22°C).

Safety Outside the Home

1. Car Safety:

- Always use a rear-facing car seat installed according to the manufacturer's instructions. Ensure that the car seat is appropriate for your baby's weight and height.
- Never leave your baby alone in a car, even for a minute.

2. Sun Protection:

- Keep your newborn out of direct sunlight. Use a stroller with a sunshade and dress your baby in lightweight, long-sleeved clothing.
- Babies under six months should avoid sunscreen; use removable mesh sunscreens on car windows or an umbrella for shade instead.

3. Handling and Holding:

- Always support your baby's head and neck when picking them up or carrying them.
- Be cautious about who holds your baby; young children should always be seated and supervised while holding a newborn.

4. Stroller Safety:

- Choose a sturdy stroller suitable for your baby's age and weight. Always use the safety harness when your baby is in the stroller.
- Be cautious with stroller accessories; heavy items can cause a stroller to tip over if hung on the handles.

General Safety Practices

1. Regular Pediatric Visits:

- Keep up with regular pediatric visits to ensure your baby is developing as expected, and to discuss any concerns you might have about their health or safety.

2. Keep Emergency Numbers Handy:

- Have a list of emergency contacts, including your pediatrician's number, local emergency services, and poison control. Keep these numbers in an easily accessible location and on your phone.

3. Learn Infant CPR and First Aid:

- Consider taking an infant CPR and first aid class. Knowing these skills can be critical in an emergency and provide peace of mind.

By adhering to these safety guidelines and continuously educating yourself on the best practices for infant safety, you can significantly reduce the risks of accidents and ensure a safer environment for your newborn both at home and when out and about.

Baby Care and Hygiene

Proper baby care and hygiene are essential for keeping your newborn healthy and happy. Here's a detailed guide on how to maintain cleanliness and prevent infections for your little one:

Daily Hygiene Practices

1. Bathing:

- Newborns don't need to be bathed daily; two to three times a week is generally sufficient until they become more mobile.
- Use a soft, clean washcloth, mild baby soap, and warm water. Always keep one hand on the baby for safety.
- Be thorough yet gentle around the baby's creases and folds, such as under the arms, behind the ears, and around the neck.

2. Skin Care:

- Newborn skin is sensitive. Use hypoallergenic and fragrance-free lotions or oils that are designed for babies.
- Watch for signs of diaper rash or dry patches and apply appropriate ointments or creams as recommended by your pediatrician.

3. Navel Care:

- Keep the umbilical cord stump clean and dry until it falls off on its own (typically within 1-3 weeks after birth).
- Fold diapers away from the stump, and only give sponge baths during this time to avoid soaking the area.

4. Diapering:

- Change diapers frequently (every 2-3 hours, or immediately after bowel movements) to prevent diaper rash.
- Clean the diaper area gently but thoroughly with baby wipes or a damp washcloth. Allow the area to air dry before putting on a new diaper.
- Apply diaper rash cream as a preventive measure if your baby's skin tends to get irritated.

Oral Hygiene

1. Gum and Tooth Care:

- Before teeth arrive, clean your baby's gums with a soft, damp cloth twice a day, especially after feedings and before bedtime.
- Once teeth appear, use a small, soft-bristled toothbrush with a tiny smear of fluoride toothpaste (the size of a grain of rice) to brush their teeth gently.

Hand Hygiene

1. Washing Hands:

- Always wash your hands before handling your baby, especially when feeding or changing diapers.
- Ensure that all caregivers and visitors wash their hands before they touch the baby to prevent the spread of infections.

Clothing and Bedding

1. Laundry:

- Wash baby's clothes, bedding, and washable toys regularly in hot water with a gentle, baby-safe detergent to remove dirt and germs.
- Ensure everything is completely dry before use to prevent the growth of mold or mildew.

General Cleanliness

1. Cleaning Baby Gear:

- Regularly clean and disinfect baby items such as bottles, pacifiers, and toys, especially those that fall on the floor or come into contact with a lot of saliva.
- Sterilize feeding equipment like bottles and nipples according to the manufacturer's instructions until the baby is at least three months old.

2. Managing Illness:

- Keep your newborn away from sick people as much as possible. Newborns have immature immune systems and are more susceptible to infections.
- If you or another caregiver are sick, wear a mask and wash hands thoroughly to minimize the risk of transmitting the illness to the baby.

Maintaining high standards of hygiene will help keep your baby safe from infections and ensure their overall well-being. Regular pediatric check-ups will help monitor your baby's health and provide further guidance on care and hygiene practices specific to your baby's needs.

Couple Exercise #7: Practice Changing a Diaper Together (with a Doll)

Practicing changing a diaper together is a practical and fun exercise for expectant parents. It helps both partners feel more prepared and confident about handling one of the most frequent tasks of newborn care. Here's how you can conduct this exercise effectively:

Step 1: Gather Your Supplies

Prepare everything you would need for a real diaper change:

- **A doll** to simulate the baby.
- **A changing mat or towel** to lay the doll on.
- **Diapers**, preferably newborn size.
- **Baby wipes** for cleaning.
- **Diaper rash cream**, to practice how to apply it.
- **A diaper disposal method**, like a small trash bin or diaper pail.

Step 2: Set Up Your Changing Area

Arrange your changing station just as you would want it when the baby arrives. This helps you think through the layout and ensure all essentials are within easy reach, promoting safety and convenience.

Step 3: Demonstrate and Practice

One partner can start by demonstrating the diaper change on the doll, step-by-step, while the other watches. Here's a simple guide to follow:

- **Lay the doll down gently** on the changing mat.
- **Open a new diaper** and place it close by.
- **Remove the doll's pants** and the dirty diaper (pretend if the doll is not equipped for this).
- **Use baby wipes** to clean the doll's diaper area, wiping from front to back.
- **Lift the doll's legs** carefully to slide the clean diaper underneath.
- **Apply a small amount of diaper rash cream** if you're simulating that scenario.
- **Secure the new diaper** snugly but ensure it's not too tight.
- **Dispose of the used diaper** properly.
- **Dress the doll back** if you removed any clothing.

Swap roles and let the other partner try the same steps, guiding them through as needed.

Step 4: Discuss and Give Feedback

After both partners have tried changing the diaper, discuss the experience:

- What felt easy or challenging?
- Are there adjustments needed in the setup of the changing station?
- How can you streamline the process to make diaper changes quicker and safer?

Step 5: Address Any Concerns

Talk about any concerns either partner might have about diaper changing or related tasks, like handling the baby's legs or cleaning. Research tips or ask your healthcare provider for advice on best practices.

Step 6: Repeat Practice

Repetition is key to becoming comfortable with baby care tasks. Plan to practice diaper changing several times before the baby arrives, trying to simulate different conditions, such as a sleepy, fussy, or squirmy baby (moving the doll around a bit to mimic this).

Step 7: Clean Up

Once you've finished practicing, make sure to clean up your area and wash your hands, even though it was just practice. This is good hygiene practice for when you are doing real diaper changes.

This exercise not only prepares you for the practical task of changing diapers but also promotes teamwork and communication between partners. It can be a playful yet educational way to prepare for the realities of parenting.

10. Resources and Support
Professional Counseling and Help

Seeking professional counseling and help is an important consideration for maintaining mental and emotional well-being, especially during times of stress or transition, such as becoming a new parent. Here's how to navigate the process of finding and utilizing professional counseling services effectively:

Recognizing the Need for Professional Help

1. Identifying Signs:

- Persistent feelings of sadness, anxiety, or emptiness
- Overwhelming fatigue or lack of energy
- Dramatic changes in appetite or sleep patterns
- Difficulty concentrating or making decisions
- Increased irritability, anger, or hostility
- Withdrawal from friends, family, and activities that used to bring joy
- Thoughts of harm to oneself or others

2. Specific Circumstances:

- Struggling with relationship issues or communication problems
- Experiencing significant life changes such as pregnancy, childbirth, or parenting challenges
- Dealing with unresolved issues from one's own upbringing or past

Finding the Right Professional

1. Types of Mental Health Professionals:

- **Psychologists:** Provide therapy and counseling to help manage mental health issues but usually do not prescribe medication.
- **Psychiatrists:** Medical doctors who can prescribe medications and also provide therapy.
- **Licensed Clinical Social Workers (LCSWs) or Licensed Professional Counselors (LPCs):** Offer counseling and therapy for a variety of issues.
- **Marriage and Family Therapists (MFTs):** Specialize in relationship and family counseling.

2. How to Find a Therapist:

- **Referrals:** Ask your primary care provider, friends, family, or colleagues for referrals. You can also ask other health professionals like obstetricians, especially for issues related to postpartum depression.

- **Online Directories:** Use professional organizations such as the American Psychological Association or local mental health associations to find licensed practitioners.

- **Insurance Provider:** Check your health insurance plan for a list of covered providers to ensure services are covered under your policy.

Making the Most of Counseling

1. Preparing for the First Session:

- Write down a list of issues and goals you wish to discuss.

- Prepare a brief history of your mental health, including any treatments or medications you've tried.

- Be open and honest; the first session is about getting to know the counselor and assessing if it's a good fit.

2. Engaging in Therapy:

- Be consistent with appointments to maximize the benefits of therapy.

- Do the homework or follow the strategies suggested by your therapist.

- Communicate openly if you feel the approach isn't working so adjustments can be made.

Evaluating Progress

1. Review Goals Regularly:

- Periodically review the goals you set with your therapist to assess progress.

- Adjust goals as needed based on new situations or changes in your condition.

2. Open Communication:

- Therapy is a two-way street. Ensure you feel comfortable speaking openly with your therapist about your thoughts and feelings.

When to Consider Changing Therapists

1. Lack of Connection:

- If you don't feel understood or comfortable after several sessions, it might be necessary to look for another therapist.

- Therapy requires a strong therapeutic alliance to be effective. If the connection isn't there, the effectiveness of therapy might be limited.

Self-Help and Support Groups

1. Complement to Professional Help:

- Consider joining support groups, either in person or online. These can provide additional emotional support and insights from others going through similar experiences.

By recognizing the need for help and actively engaging in the process, professional counseling can provide significant support and tools to navigate complex emotional landscapes, leading to improved mental health and quality of life.

Recognizing and Addressing Postpartum Depression (for Both Mother and Father)

Postpartum depression (PPD) is a serious mental health condition that can affect both mothers and fathers after the birth of a child. Recognizing the symptoms and seeking timely treatment is crucial for the well-being of the entire family. Here's how to identify, address, and manage postpartum depression:

Recognizing Postpartum Depression

Symptoms in Mothers and Fathers:

- **Persistent Sadness or Low Mood:** Feeling down, tearful, or hopeless for extended periods.
- **Loss of Interest or Pleasure:** Lack of interest in activities once enjoyed, including care for the newborn.
- **Changes in Appetite and Sleep Patterns:** Significant increase or decrease in appetite; insomnia or excessive sleeping.
- **Fatigue or Loss of Energy:** Feeling tired all the time, even after resting or sleeping.
- **Feelings of Worthlessness or Guilt:** Excessive guilt, especially related to parenting or personal shortcomings.
- **Anxiety:** Intense worries about the baby's health or irrational fears about parenting competency.
- **Withdrawal from Social Activities:** Pulling away from friends and family and avoiding social interactions.
- **Thoughts of Harming Yourself or the Baby:** These are severe symptoms that require immediate medical attention.

Addressing Postpartum Depression

1. Acknowledge the Feelings:

- Recognize that postpartum depression is a medical condition, not a weakness or failure. It can happen to anyone and is not the fault of the affected person.

2. Seek Professional Help:

- Consult with a healthcare provider as soon as symptoms are noticed. Early intervention can lead to better outcomes. Treatment may include counseling, support groups, and possibly medication.

3. Support from Partners and Family:

- Partners and family members play a critical role in support and recovery. They should be attentive, provide emotional support, and help with the baby and household tasks to reduce stress on the parent experiencing PPD.

Management and Treatment

1. Therapy:

- **Cognitive Behavioral Therapy (CBT) and Interpersonal Therapy (IPT):** Proven effective for treating PPD. These therapies help address negative thought patterns and improve interpersonal relationships and support systems.

2. Medication:

- Antidepressants may be prescribed by a healthcare provider. For breastfeeding mothers, there are safe options that won't harm the baby.

3. Lifestyle Adjustments:

- Regular physical activity, a healthy diet, and sufficient sleep can improve symptoms. Encourage small, manageable amounts of activity as approved by a healthcare provider.

4. Support Groups:

- Joining a support group can provide validation and encouragement from others who understand the challenges of PPD.

5. Self-Care:

- Encourage self-care practices that reduce stress and increase relaxation, such as mindfulness, meditation, or hobbies that bring joy.

6. Education:

- Both parents should educate themselves about PPD to understand the symptoms, treatments, and recovery processes. This knowledge can demystify many fears and misconceptions about the condition.

Preventing Isolation

- Encourage connections with friends, family, or others, which can provide emotional support and reduce feelings of isolation and loneliness.

Continuous Monitoring

- Monitor the progress of treatment closely and maintain regular check-ins with healthcare providers. Adjust treatments as needed, based on responses and changes in symptoms.

Understanding that postpartum depression is a treatable condition can help remove the stigma and encourage affected parents to seek the necessary help. With the right support and treatment, parents can recover from PPD and fully enjoy their new roles.

Building a Family and Social Support Network

Building a strong family and social support network is crucial for emotional well-being, particularly during significant life transitions like welcoming a new baby. Here's how you can create and strengthen a support network that sustains and uplifts your family.

Identify Potential Support Members

1. Family Members:

- Close family can provide emotional and practical support. Identify family members who can be relied upon for childcare, household tasks, or simply as trusted confidants.

2. Friends:

- Friends, especially those with parenting experience or those going through similar life stages, can offer invaluable support, advice, and empathy.

3. Neighbors:

- Cultivating relationships with neighbors can provide a sense of community and safety. Neighbors can offer quick help or company, and in some cases, may become close, reliable friends.

4. Community or Religious Groups:

- Being part of community centers, religious groups, or clubs can widen your support network. These groups often provide activities and resources for families and children, fostering a sense of belonging and community support.

Strengthen Your Network

1. Be Proactive:

- Don't wait for others to reach out. Take the initiative to invite family or friends over, join local groups, or participate in community events.

2. Use Technology:

- Utilize social media, messaging apps, or online forums to stay connected with distant family members and friends. Online parenting groups can also be a great resource for advice and support.

3. Offer Support:

- A support network is a two-way street. Be ready to offer your support to others in your network when they need it. This reciprocity strengthens relationships and ensures mutual aid.

4. Regular Communication:

- Keep regular contact with your network through calls, texts, emails, or social media. Consistent communication helps maintain strong connections and keeps others informed about your life and needs.

Leverage Community Resources

1. Parenting Classes and Workshops:

- Many community centers, hospitals, and schools offer classes and workshops for new parents. These can be great places to learn and meet other parents.

2. Support Groups:

- Join support groups for parents where experiences and challenges can be shared in a supportive environment, offering both emotional relief and practical advice.

3. Professional Services:

- Identify and connect with professional services in your area, such as counselors, pediatricians, and lactation consultants, who can provide expert support.

Maintaining the Network

1. Schedule Regular Meetups:

- Plan regular gatherings or activities, like monthly dinners or group outings, to keep the network active and engaged.

2. Celebrate Together:

- Celebrate milestones, holidays, and successes together. This strengthens bonds and creates lasting memories.

3. Adapt the Network Over Time:

- As your family's needs change, so too might your support network. New members may join while others might take a step back depending on circumstances. Be open to this natural evolution.

Handling Challenges

1. Set Boundaries:

- It's important to establish healthy boundaries with members of your support network to prevent feelings of overwhelm or intrusion into family life.

2. Communicate Needs Clearly:

- Be clear about what type of support you need. Whether it's practical help like babysitting or emotional support, communicating your needs clearly can prevent misunderstandings.

Building and maintaining a supportive social network is vital for navigating the challenges and joys of parenting. It not only helps in practical terms but also enriches your family's life with stronger emotional connections and a broader sense of community.

Couple Exercise #8: Find and Join a Local or Online Support Group

Joining a support group can be incredibly beneficial for couples, especially new parents who might be navigating the complexities of parenting together for the first time. Here's a step-by-step guide to help you find and join a local or online support group as a couple:

Step 1: Identify Your Needs

Discuss with your partner what you both hope to gain from joining a support group. Are you looking for parenting advice, emotional support, or simply the opportunity to connect with other parents who are experiencing similar challenges? Understanding your needs will help guide your search for the right group.

Step 2: Research Options

Local Groups:

- Check with local hospitals, pediatric offices, and community centers, which often host or can recommend support groups for parents.
- Visit local libraries or family resource centers, as they often have information on parent groups and other community programs.

Online Groups:

- Look for parenting forums and groups on social media platforms such as Facebook, Reddit, or specialized parenting websites.
- Consider apps and online platforms dedicated to parenting and family support, like Peanut, BabyCenter, and Circle of Moms, where you can connect with others digitally.

Step 3: Evaluate the Group

Once you've found a few potential groups, consider the following:

- **Group Focus:** Does the group's focus align with your needs? Some groups might center around specific aspects of parenting, like breastfeeding or postpartum recovery.
- **Meeting Schedule:** Does the group meet at times you both can attend? Consider your daily routines and other commitments.
- **Group Size and Composition:** Do you prefer a smaller, more intimate group or a larger, more diverse one?
- **Moderation and Structure:** Is the group facilitated by a professional? Groups led by therapists or social workers can provide a structured environment that might be beneficial for discussing sensitive issues.

Step 4: Attend a Session

Most groups will allow you to attend a meeting before fully committing. Visit a group session to see how the group operates and if the dynamics fit your expectations:

- **Participate Actively:** Engage in the discussions to get a real feel for the group's supportive environment.
- **Observe Interactions:** Pay attention to how members interact and how the moderators handle discussions.

Step 5: Discuss Your Impressions

After attending a session, discuss your thoughts with your partner:

- Did you feel welcomed and supported?
- Were the discussions relevant and helpful?
- Do you think the group could meet your needs as a couple?

Step 6: Commit to Participation

If you've found a group that feels like a good fit, commit to participating regularly. Consistent involvement can lead to stronger connections and more meaningful support.

Step 7: Re-evaluate as Needed

As you grow in your parenting journey, your needs might change. Periodically re-evaluate whether the support group still meets your needs, or if you should look for another group that aligns with your current situation.

Step 8: Create Your Own Group

If you don't find what you're looking for, consider starting your own support group. You can set the focus, structure, and schedule that best fit your needs, and invite others from your community or online network to join.

Joining a support group can provide both practical parenting tips and emotional support, helping to strengthen your relationship as you navigate the challenges of parenting together. It's also a wonderful way to make lifelong friends who share similar experiences and challenges.

FAQ

Welcome to the FAQ chapter! Here, we've compiled a list of some of the most common questions we've received from new parents, along with straightforward answers to help clarify and provide support as you navigate the exciting and sometimes challenging journey of parenthood.

Q1: How often should a newborn be fed?

A1: Newborns typically need to be fed every 2-3 hours, amounting to about 8-12 feedings over 24 hours. Watch for signs of hunger such as fussing, mouthing, and rooting, and try to feed before your baby starts crying.

Q2: What are the signs of a good latch during breastfeeding?

A2: A good latch means your baby has a large portion of the lower areola (the area around the nipple) in their mouth, and the latch is comfortable without pain. You should see the baby's jaw moving, and possibly hear swallowing. If it hurts, break the suction and try again.

Q3: When can I start sleep training my baby?

A3: Many experts suggest waiting until the baby is around 4 to 6 months old before starting formal sleep training, as they're developmentally able to sleep through the night without needing to eat. Always consult with your pediatrician to determine the best time and method for your baby.

Q4: What are the best ways to soothe a crying baby?

A4: Soothing a crying baby can involve various strategies: swaddling, shushing, swinging gently, giving a pacifier, or holding the baby on their side or stomach while supporting their head. Sometimes a change of scenery, a car ride, or simply cuddling closely can help.

Q5: How do I know if my baby is getting enough to eat?

A5: Signs that your baby is eating enough include regular weight gain (your pediatrician will help you know if your baby is on track), about six wet diapers a day, and at least three bowel movements a day in the first few weeks.

Q6: When should I worry about a fever?

A6: For newborns and young babies, a rectal temperature of 100.4°F (38°C) or higher warrants a call to your doctor. In infants, even a slight fever can be a sign of a serious infection.

Q7: How can I help my baby develop good sleep habits?

A7: Establishing a bedtime routine can significantly aid in developing good sleep habits. The routine might include a bath, a story, and some quiet time before putting your baby to bed while they're drowsy but awake. Consistency is key.

Q8: Is it normal for my baby to have irregular bowel movements?

A8: Yes, it's normal for babies, especially those who are breastfed, to have irregular bowel movements. Some might have a bowel movement every feeding; others might go several days without one. As long as the baby is not uncomfortable, this is typically fine.

Q9: How can I ensure my baby's safety in the car?

A9: Always use a rear-facing car seat placed in the back seat of your vehicle. Ensure the car seat is installed correctly (most local fire stations will check this for free) and that the harnesses are snug against the baby's chest.

Q10: When should my baby start solid foods?

A10: Most babies are ready to start solid foods around six months old, but it can vary. Signs your baby is ready include being able to sit up with minimal support, showing curiosity about what you are eating, and the ability to reject food by turning their head away.

Concluding Thoughts and Acknowledgements

As we come to the conclusion of this guide, it is important to pause and reflect on the journey we have taken together. Becoming a parent is one of life's most profound transformations, full of challenges, joys and continuous learning. Each page of this book has been crafted with the hope of making the transition to parenthood a little easier and a lot more informed.

Embracing the journey

Parenting is not a destination, but a journey that is unique to each individual. As you have learned in the various chapters, there are techniques and knowledge that can prepare you, but much of parenting comes from the heart and intuition. Trust yourself, lean into your new knowledge and embrace every moment with your child.

Continuous learning

Remember that learning does not stop at the last page of this book. As your child grows, so does your experience and understanding. Remain curious, seek advice when needed, and continue to attend parenting communities. The landscapes of parenting are constantly evolving, and keeping informed is the best tool for dealing with them.

Gratitude and thanks

This book would not have been possible without the contributions and insights of a number of dedicated individuals. First, a heartfelt thank you to the clinicians, counselors and educators whose expertise enriches these pages. Your dedication to the well-being of families around the world is deeply appreciated.

To my family, thank you for your unceasing support and encouragement. Your belief in the importance of this project has been a constant source of motivation.

And finally, to you readers, thank you for entrusting this book to your parenting journey. May the chapters you have explored provide you with confidence and comfort as you face one of life's most important roles.

Looking ahead

As you move forward, remember that no book has all the answers, and that's okay. Every child is different and each day offers new opportunities to learn and grow together. Appreciate the small moments, look for joy in the challenges, and always give yourself grace.

Thank you for allowing this book to accompany you through the early stages of your incredible journey as parents. May the road ahead be filled with love, laughter and the joyful discovery of the world through your child's eyes.

Happy parenting!

SCAN THE QR CODE

OR COPY THE FOLLOWING URL:
https://bit.ly/4fH9Yl4

NOTES

Pin your appointments, schedules and questions here to keep track of them

Made in United States
Orlando, FL
25 October 2024